Our Padre

The Inspiring Life and Stories of Fr. Kilian Dreiling, C.PP.S. WWII Army Chaplain

Joseph J. Frey

5/2/09

Printing Partners, Inc.

Author: Joseph S. Smith
Graphic Designer: Steven Larracey
Publishing Director: Joel O'Brien
Copyright ©2004 Joseph S. Smith
Second Printing

Printed in the United States of America

Printing Partners
929 W. 16th Street
Indianapolis, IN 46202
www.printingpartners.net

ISBN: 0-9725960-3-8

Our Padre: The Inspiring Life and Stories of Fr. Kilian Dreiling, C.PP.S. — WWII Army Chaplain

Books available at www.ourpadre.com

Dedication

This book is dedicated to my Mom and Dad,
Marcella B. and Joseph T. Smith.

Thanks for giving me the greatest gift I will ever receive;
the gift of faith.

Acknowledgements

I am deeply grateful to the many friends of Fr. Kilian Dreiling, family members, clergymen and former fellow soldiers who contributed not only numerous documents and letters, but oral histories as well. While the list of those who have provided support and encouragement is too numerous to mention here, there are several whose contributions were instrumental in helping me fill in the canvas of Fr. Kilian Dreiling's life.

To my parents, Joseph T. "Smitty" Smith and Marcella B. Smith, I am deeply indebted. Dad and Mom were instrumental in soliciting information from members of the 92nd Evacuation Hospital and in gathering numerous reference documents. In addition, Mom transcribed all of Fr. Kilian's sermons from the 92nd Evacuation Hospital reunions from audiotapes to paper. It is indeed a luxury to have an eyewitness to Fr. Kilian's influential war years only a telephone call away, and Dad's recollections of the events in this book were an invaluable contribution. In addition, my parents' encouragement and excitement for this project kept me going numerous times when I needed it.

Without Fr. Paul Link's two books about the chaplains of the C.PP.S. Priests, "For God and Country," books one and two, many of Fr. Kilian's eyewitness accounts of his WWII years would have been lost to history. Fr. Link's books also provided excellent reference material for developing a deeper understanding of the challenges facing wartime chaplains. I highly recommend these readings for anyone who wishes to explore the subject of WWII army chaplains at greater length. I would also like to thank Brother Jude, C.PP.S. at St. Charles Center in Carthagena, OH for his assistance in sending along Fr. Kilian's personal effects and records, and for contributing his own personal memories.

Mrs. Agnes Pfannenstiel, Fr. Kilian's cousin and former parish secretary was an invaluable link to Fr. Kilian's post-war, pastoral years in Wakeeney, KS. I hope this book will help refresh her own "storehouse full of memories."

To all of the veterans of the 92nd Evacuation Hospital who

enthusiastically contributed your memories and reflections of Fr. Kilian, thank you for providing greater depth to the story of an American hero. To Elsie Schneider, Fr. Joseph Nassal and to the many others who helped fill in the canvas with information about Fr. Kilian's life before and after the war, I am very grateful for your valuable contribution to this effort.

Without the patience and understanding of my wife Ginny, I would never have been able to devote the time necessary to complete this effort. Without her support and devotion to our four children, I could never have finished this project.

Finally, I believe I speak for all of those who were blessed to have known and loved Fr. Kilian Dreiling when I say, "Thank you Fr. Kilian for teaching us how to love our fellow man, how to speak the truth with conviction, and how to live our beautiful faith in Jesus Christ."

Introduction

St. Charles Center is nestled in western Ohio near the town of Carthagena. Like many former Catholic seminaries today, the men who walk its hallways are no longer young and full of mischief. Many require the assistance of a walker, cane or motorized wheelchair. Yet, the echoes of the boisterous and hopeful young seminarians who grew from boys to men here can still be heard.

In one corner of the cemetery at St. Charles lie the graves of over 60 Catholic military chaplains. These men bravely served their country in each American conflict from the Civil War to Vietnam. The amazing stories of the lives of these men are largely, lost to history. However, one of these remarkable men, Fr. Kilian Dreiling, recorded the most memorable and amazing events of his life into a captivating series of short stories.

Few people have witnessed so much of both the brutality and the beauty of this past century, as has Fr. Kilian Dreiling. While he was never famous, he earned the admiration and love of thousands of people whose lives he touched. He was in his mid-30's when he served as a WWII army chaplain, and was considered an "old man" by the young GIs to which he ministered. However, he quickly earned their undying respect and devotion. This devotion would be lifelong.

Men and women of the 92nd Evacuation Hospital recall how Fr. Kilian braved enemy fire in order to offer comfort to suffering men in their final hours. He also provided strength and spiritual direction to thousands of scared and confused American men and boys. After the war, he heard the confessions of Nazi concentration camp guards, and would later follow through on promises that he had made to dying soldiers by visiting their parents and loved ones. By relating his first-hand accounts of each son's death, Fr. Killian was forced to relive, over and over again, the tragic ending of a precious life, cut short by war. This he did willingly, in order to bring some closure and a measure of comfort to the grieving parents.

As an anti-Communist lecturer, Fr. Kilian helped educate a naïve American public to the evils and dangers of this Godless and dehumanizing ideology. As a parish pastor he was a wise yet firm shepherd, inspiring his flock each Sunday with riveting and emotionally charged sermons, very often drawn from his wartime experiences. His outstanding military service record and personal charm afforded Fr. Kilian the opportunity to meet many influential figures of his time, including Pope Pious XII, Douglas MacArthur, Old Queen Mary of England and many others.

What makes the story of Fr. Kilian so compelling and important for future generations however, is his message of hope. Fr. Kilian displayed the rare ability to see God's hand in all things, while putting the remarkable events of the twentieth century into perspective for us. He possessed in great measure, qualities that the "Greatest Generation" valued above all: Courage, compassion and self-sacrifice, faith, hope and love for our fellow man. His story is too remarkable and inspiring not to be told.

I will never forget the day that my father returned home from his first army reunion with a tall, skinny, elderly Catholic priest. While this man was a total stranger to us, he had the warmest smile I had ever seen. It had been 30 years since the end of WWII, yet none of my brothers and sisters or I could recall our father even once mentioning the army chaplain from his unit. Fr. Kilian Dreiling seemed different from the other priests that we knew. His physical appearance was striking. Nearly 70, he still had a commanding presence and a booming voice, which regularly broke into laughter.

At age 16, I was not easily impressed. However, I became totally captivated by this man and his wonderful stories. He had been all over the world and he knew so many famous people! He seemed to me, a living link to nearly every significant historical event of the 20th century. In time, we would also learn of his great capacity for love and compassion. Thus began a lifelong friendship between our family and Fr. Kilian Dreiling.

Fortunately, Fr. Kilian left us a written record of his most important life experiences. He was an excellent storyteller, and he eventually committed his favorites to paper. His powerful sermons helped him perfect these stories over time. This rich legacy represents the heart and soul of this book. Fr. Kilian speaks to us even today through these stories. I have attempted to weave them together in chronological order with historical perspective.

Every generation needs heroes. For thousands of us who were fortunate enough to know Fr. Kilian Dreiling, he was ours. He is an example of one person who made a difference in the lives of many others by providing inspiration, courage and hope at a time when it was needed most. I hope and pray that in some small way, Fr. Kilian's life and his beautiful stories may touch your heart, as they have touched mine.

Chapter 1

Confession of "The Beast"

Fr. Kilian Dreiling was in his late thirties when he was stationed in post WWII occupied Germany in 1946. He had had many close calls as a chaplain in General Douglas MacArthur's 6th U.S. Army, surviving the New Guinea and Philippine campaigns. His military record was outstanding and by now he had been promoted to the rank of Major. Yet while the rest of his outfit, the 92nd Evacuation Hospital, had been mustered out of the service, Kilian re-enlisted and was transferred to Germany after a short leave home.

Fr. Kilian's services were still greatly needed. In addition to being a trusted officer with a performance rating of 5.9 out of 6.0, Fr. Kilian's first language was German. In fact, as the son of first generation immigrants, he spoke little English until the age of 14 when he entered the seminary in Ohio.

There were hundreds of thousands of allied troops in Europe and the situation was still quite volatile. Many U.S. officers were talking openly of the need to push the Russian Army out of Europe, and both the Americans and Russians were busy gathering as much intelligence as possible from the captured Nazis. Many feared that war with the Soviet Union was inevitable. Western Europe, devastated from six years of total, all-out war, was fertile ground for the communist seeds now being sown by the Soviets.

In this environment, Fr. Kilian Dreiling was ministering not only to thousands of U.S. troops, but to local Germans and Austrians as well. His language skills, tenacity and personal charm were invaluable as he served in a liaison capacity with local officials and as "morale officer" for the American GIs. He had every reason to be proud of his accomplishments. He had witnessed a great deal more in his less than 40 years on Earth than most could imagine in a lifetime. He saw the aftermath of Japanese atrocities, experienced Kamikaze attacks and invasions, and suffered from debilitating jungle diseases. In addition, one of his most daunting challenges was the exhaustive task of burying thousands of young American soldiers.

Fr. Kilian Dreiling was a man tested by the fires of war who had become much stronger and compassionate as a result. Yet, he was never soured by these experiences. He always seemed to have hope, a commodity that he freely dispensed to others. He had become a more deeply spiritual man, and had reached a level of excellence in the profession of "U.S. Army Chaplain" attained by very few.

For these reasons, Fr. Kilian was selected for a top-secret mission. However, even he could not have been totally prepared for what was about to happen. Fr. Kilian tells this story in his own words.

The "Beast of Dachau"

The forward thrust of this assignment is the infinitely powerful cause and prompt effect of a sincere devotion to the Precious Blood of Jesus. I hope to accomplish this by employing the simple method of the greatest storyteller of all time, namely, Jesus of Nazareth.

Because I was woefully lacking in points, the army offered to send me to the states immediately after V.J. Day for 45 days, provided that I would agree to return to Japan for further occupational duty. I agreed in writing to this arrangement.

After 45 days of vacation in the states, I found myself clinging to the rail of a transport ship destined not for Japan but for Europe. When I arrived, I found Western Europe not only devastated but pulverized. The sight was ghastly and grim. In retrospect, insanely wasteful and dreadfully sad. For me, this duty had still another aspect; it was the coldest winter in Heidelberg in 50 years.

Malaria, amoebic dysentery and battle fatigue became my constant and persistent companions. Time and again I appealed to return stateside to recuperate, only to find myself holding on to yet another rail, not for the United States but to some ten different countries on what was called a "recuperation basis."

Chaplain Medeaux was the area chaplain. He finally released me after I agreed to conduct 28 missions at all our military installations. It

was after a series of missions that I returned to home base, Frankfurt, for a few days rest. Six Catholic chaplains lived in one house. I had not even closed the front door when Fr. Rush, the base chaplain, told me to report to headquarters promptly at 0900 the next morning.

The next morning I stood at the colonel's door. He looked up from his paper and said, "Father, sit down." When he finally finished the work at hand, he looked at me and spoke almost apologetically. "Father, we are sending you on a top secret mission. Only you and I, and a few men on my staff know where you will go and what you will do. The mission is so secret that even if the slightest part is leaked, we will know it came from you." I told him I had ample experience in keeping the seal of confession. For the first time he smiled and said, "You are right father, I got the right man."

The next morning, I again stood at attention in the colonel's office. He called in my driver, showed him the map, and where he would be taking me. After the driver left, the colonel gave me further instructions. "After some 30 to 40 miles you will be stopped, your driver and jeep will be confiscated, and you will be transferred to a command car. From there you will take orders from the command car."

All this and more actually happened. I was not only transferred to the command car, I was frisked and my Mass kit was searched. I was no longer allowed to speak to my driver. After driving still another 30 or 40 miles I saw in the distance a tremendous complex on the outskirts of a forest. I suspected it was a prison camp. When we neared the camp, the huge iron gates swung open and I was suddenly caught in the jaws of what might be described as a dark hole.

Sandwiched between two guards, we were led by a sergeant to a large room. I was told to set up my Mass kit. As I set up for Mass, only one prisoner came in. I protested strongly, saying that I had 9,000 soldiers back in Frankfurt and had promised Fr. Rush that I would have 6:00 Mass for them. The sergeant told me he would see what he could do. One more prisoner finally came and when I repeated my protest to the sergeant, he took me to the far end of the room and whispered, "Father, the prisoners here are of such a dangerous nature that they will never permit more than two in the same room at the same time."

After Mass with these two prisoners, I looked at my watch, hoping I could still make Frankfurt in time for the 6:00 Mass. But the sergeant approached me and said, "Father, we have 17 prisoners who demand to see a Catholic chaplain. I will lead you from cell to cell." I no longer protested and simply followed him.

The prisoners were of all nationalities and religious convictions. Language was a barrier. Long after I should have been in Frankfurt, I took a deep sigh of relief. The ordeal, I thought, was over. But once more the sergeant approached me and said, "Now Father, we have one more prisoner to see. For three days and nights, she has screamed hysterically to see a Catholic priest. She is not a Catholic, but insisted on her Geneva rights to see you."

Since the sergeant had described the prisoner as "she," I asked him as he led me to her cell, "This would not be the 'Beast' of Dachau would it?" The sergeant simply nodded and before I could protest, we were at her cell. The guards physically pushed me into the cell and closed the door behind me. When I looked around to see what protection I had, I saw two bayonets sticking through the peephole. One guard comforted me by saying, "Father, don't worry. We will protect you."

In front of me, stretched out on a concrete floor, lay this terrible creature in utter, unbelievable despair. Without so much as raising her head, she demanded in a low, guttural voice, "You are a Catholic priest?"

"I am."

"Prove it." Her German was excellent.

"What precisely do you want me to say to prove that I am a Catholic priest?"

"Say the Ave in Latin," she said. I did.

"Now say the confiteor in Latin." Every altar boy knows that this is, of all prayers, the most difficult, but I said it to her satisfaction.

Then she put me in a real bind. "Now give me the words of absolution in Latin," she said. I hesitated for a minute but obliged her, even with my reservations.

Now raising her head slightly, she literally trounced on me. She cursed me, ridiculed me, scoffed at me, and denounced me in the most correct German, but in the most terrible language. Over and over she screamed, "I am damned! I am damned! My father cursed me, my mother cursed me, every innocent prisoner I led to his death cursed me! Yes, the prisoners I slowly tortured to death cursed me a thousand times over!" Staring at me with a diabolical look, she said, "What makes you foolish enough to think that you can forgive my sins when not even God has the power to forgive me?"

When she was near total exhaustion from this tirade, she forcefully thrust her hands into my face and screamed, "You damn fool! Can't you see the blood of thousands of innocent prisoners dripping from my hands? I am cursed! I am damned forever!"

I now took the lead. "Olga (not her real name), I cannot see the blood of a thousand prisoners dripping from your hands, but I can see the Precious Blood of Jesus dripping from the cross. I do not condone your sins, many as the sands of the seashore and red and scarlet. My memories of Dachau are deeply imprinted. I was there only a week ago. Yes, I saw the shelves and shelves of souvenirs made out of the skins of prisoners. I saw your ghastly work. I saw the crematories, the underground rooms full to the ceiling with urns containing the ashes of dead prisoners. Even more horrible, I saw the kennels where you detained and starved dogs and then stood by the gate and watched the hungry dogs tear dozens of prisoners to pieces. I saw the grave that contained some 30,000 of the noble dead. I saw all that and much more.

"But let me remind you that your greatest sin is the arrogance, your diabolical pride, your terrible boast that God does not have the power to undo what Olga has done; forgive her sins. You want to go down in history for all to see and know that Olga did something that God cannot undo and therefore Olga is more powerful than God. I repeat, your sins are horrible but the most heinous is your pride, your arrogance, your boast, your despair!

"Yes, you see the blood of a thousand innocent prisoners dripping from your hands, then why not see the Precious Blood of Jesus dripping from the cross? The blood of Jesus redeemed all mankind. If the Precious Blood of Jesus could redeem the sins of all the world, how dare you say, how dare you boast, that it is not powerful enough to cleanse the sins of one individual!

"I now challenge you, like the good thief, repent! And like him, you may see the kingdom of God, if not today then certainly in the future. Acknowledge your crimes humbly and sorrowfully and learn that God is infinitely merciful and forgiving. Weep for your sins and like Peter you will say, 'Not by worthless silver and gold but by the Precious of Christ you were redeemed.'"

Most unexpectedly, Olga collapsed. She broke into uncontrollable sobbing that seemed to shake even the concrete floor of her cell. Over and over she now pleaded, "Herr Fadder bitte ueber-setsen, ueber-setsen." (Please repeat, repeat, translate again.) And finally she exclaimed, "It is true, yes it is true. God is infinitely powerful and infinitely merciful." Slowly she scuffled back to her cot on her knees. I watched her and even wept with her. I so completely and gratefully agreed with her. After awhile, I left.

Before leaving the complex, I asked the sergeant to take me back to her cell. I looked through the peephole and there she sat on her cot like a Grecian, marble statue. She repeated over and over, "It is true, God is merciful and infinitely powerful." A second time I left her, never to see her again.

The trip back to Frankfurt was long and I had ample time to think. And the thought that remains with me even today is what human cleverness or worldly wisdom cannot accomplish, the Precious Blood of Jesus did. For certainly it was the Precious Blood that produced this miraculous effect, the conversion of Olga. *

---

* The infamous "Beast of Dachau" was almost certainly Ilse Koch, the wife of Buchenwald death camp Commandant Karl Otto Koch. After the war, Ilse Koch was the most notorious war criminal brought before the U.S. military tribunal held at Dachau in the Spring of 1947. An American reporter who was covering the tribunal gave Ilse Koch the nickname the "Bitch of Buchenwald". Accused of, among other heinous crimes, ordering the murder of prisoners so that she could have their tattooed skin made into lampshades, she was never convicted of this charge. Fr. Kilian most likely changed her nickname to "Beast of Dachau," along with her real name, to honor the seal of confession. Ilse Koch was sentenced to life in prison and eventually committed suicide in her cell in 1967, some 20 years later. [2]

The confession of the "Beast of Dachau" made a profound impression upon Fr. Kilian Dreiling. It was a story that he told often, with perhaps more than a little pride. Fr. Kilian used the story of Christ's redemptive, saving grace, prevailing over one of Satan's most evil, captive souls as a powerful teaching tool. He was after all, a missionary, who needed to inspire his audience quickly. He found that powerful stories were a great way to engage his audience, not unlike the carpenter whose teachings he preached.

Fr. Kilian admits his own apprehension at the sudden prospect of a face-to-face encounter with evil incarnate. Perhaps he saw this as the ultimate test for a Catholic priest. Here was a woman who as an SS "Aufseherin," (female overseer)[2], and wife of the camp Commandant, starved guard dogs in order to watch them devour screaming prisoners. She had also been accused of selecting prisoners with "interesting tattoos" to be murdered so that their skin could be made into lampshades. Now, Fr. Kilian was in a position to *absolve her for her sins!*

In this encounter, Fr. Kilian triumphs because of the strength of his own faith. While readily admitting his own fears upon facing such an evil soul, he truly believed that his God, all loving and all-knowing, could forgive even the worst sinner. As it turned out, the "Beast" was unprepared to stand up to the faith of Fr. Kilian. She collapsed and wept because for one brief moment, he had touched her cold heart. He had allowed her to believe, at least for that moment, that there could be something deep inside her worth loving in the eyes of God. Faith like Fr. Kilian's was rare in Nazi Germany.

In many ways, this event became a defining moment in Fr. Kilian's life. He had stared evil right in the eye, and evil blinked! What kind of man could do this? A very rare one indeed.

Fr. Kilian Dreiling was a complex man driven by simple, straightforward principles. During the 90 years of his incredibly rich and full life, he became a revered Catholic priest, a humanitarian, a scholar and a patriot. Among the members of the 92nd Evacuation Hospital and the 239th Engineering Battalion during WWII, his many parishioners, religious brethren and his friends and family, Fr. Kilian was legendary. He was known for his humor, his unshakeable faith and dedication, his loyalty, his fearlessness, and for his ability to inspire, encourage and lead others. He was a powerful and positive influence on the lives of many thousands during his lifetime.

Fr. Kilian was famous for his powerful sermons. Like the man whose teachings he followed, he spoke in parables. His wartime experiences and his variety of assignments in many years as a Catholic Priest had exposed him to the very best and the very worst that mankind had to offer. His own personal tragedies made him stronger and more resilient, yet they also taught him compassion. Fr. Kilian was an accomplished and published writer who wove these experiences into inspiring and thought-provoking stories that became the basis for many of his sermons. He would allow his audience to experience the entire spectrum of human emotions. He could make parishioners laugh out loud, then suddenly command their attention with his booming voice. When he chose, he could also move his entire audience to tears.

Fr. Kilian carried himself with the quiet confidence and demeanor of a man who knew his purpose in life. Tall of stature, he had a commanding presence. His life was a legacy of faith: Faith in God, in the adopted country of his parents and in his fellow man.

While many were in awe of Fr. Kilian's seemingly endless talents, dedication and energy, it is important to remember that he was also very human. He relished the company of friends and family. He enjoyed cooking for his guests (Kilian was a marvelous cook), and he was energized by stimulating conversation. A very "down-to-earth" person, he had a gift for seeing the good in all people.

An army nurse would later say of Fr. Kilian, "If Fr. Kilian were God, everybody would go to heaven." [1]

Chapter 2

From Russia to the Windswept Plains of Kansas

A major reason why Fr. Kilian Dreiling had been assigned to the occupying U.S. Army in Germany after WWII was the fact that he spoke fluent German. He did not just speak it. He was German. To be more specific, Kilian was a Russian-German American (this is how he described his own ancestry).

Michael and Agnes (Kuhn) Dreiling, Kilian's parents, emigrated from Russia's Volga region to the United States in the late 1800's to avoid persecution and military conscription.[1] They settled on the windswept plains of Kansas, along with thousands of other "Volga Russians," where they quickly adapted to their new culture and nationality. That they adapted so well and so quickly is surprising, considering how rigidly they clung to their German culture and language for over 100 years while living in Russia.[2]

The Dreiling family, along with hundreds of thousands of other Germans had immigrated to Russia over 100 years earlier. Lured by Catherine the Great, Empress of Russia, immigrants from many different German principalities fled persecution and mandatory military service under Frederick the Great. In Russia, they were promised freedom of religion, the opportunity to preserve their German language and culture, and exemption from military service.[2]

Catherine was looking for settlers to populate the wild Volga region and to serve as a buffer zone between "civilized" Russia and the marauding "Kirghiz" tribes of the Steppe region. The "Volga Germans" faced tremendous hardships on the Steppes. They were subjected to raids during which whole towns might be massacred. Many of their young were carried off and lived the rest of their lives as Kirghiz tribesmen.

All of these hardships, along with an unusual amount of freedom for the time, helped shape a uniquely German cultural "island" within Russia. Volga Germans, while officially Russian citizens, were very independent and still very German. Most were farmers and tradesmen, and the faith that they developed was unusually strong. Most were staunch Catholics, but many were also rather superstitious, living in constant fear of barbaric Kirghiz "boogeymen".[2]

Catherine kept her word and until the late 1800's, Volga Germans were exempt from conscripted military service. This changed however in the 1870's when Czar Alexander II revoked all privileges accorded to the Volga Germans. Fr. Herbert Linenberger, a cousin of Fr. Kilian, explains what happened next.

"The dreaded prospect of military service, the loss of self-government and the 'Russianization' of their schools and way of life created a shock wave of distrust that impelled our ancestors to seek more friendly countries to harbor them. They turned to North and South America..."[3]

Those who left would write family and friends telling them about the suitability of their new land for settlement. One of the areas that received high marks was Western Kansas. The wild, flat and windswept plains were reminiscent of the Volga region in Russia, and the hearty wheat the immigrants brought with them thrived on the windy plains.[2]

Victoria, Kansas was one area where they began to congregate, and Kilian's parents settled here on a small farm. In America, the Volga Germans adapted quickly. The first generation born to these immigrants would call themselves "Americans", and many were quick to volunteer to fight for their new country against their ancestral homeland in WWI. The irony is that the ancestors of these Americans had fled not once, but twice to escape military conscription. Three of Kilian's older brothers fought in WWI, and their stories helped fuel a lifelong patriotism within Kilian.

Michael and Agnes Dreiling were strong Catholics who considered themselves very blessed to have 17 children. Kilian was the 10th of these children and the fifth son. He grew up in an environment short on material possessions but rich in faith. When Kilian was born his father prayed that God would grant him "faith that would wash."

Michael Dreiling wanted Kilian to develop the kind of faith that wouldn't "wash out," like most of the home-made dyes that the people of the plains commonly used to dye their own clothes. [4]

The Dreiling family children were blessed with above average height and were given names that sound very strange to us today. The fact that most of them eventually "Americanized" their names with shorter, American-sounding nicknames suggests that their names probably sounded strange, even to Americans of the early 20th century. Here are the names of Agnes and Michael's children, along with their year of birth: Aquilinus, or "Ack" (1894), Raymond, who at 6' 4" tall was called "Langa" Ryemund (1896), Bernard or "Ben" (1897), Hieronymus or "Jerry" (1898), Margaret (1900), Euphrosena or "Sena" (1902), Odillia, who later became Sister Virginta (1903), Armella (1904), Ada (1906), Kilian (1907), Sophia or "Sophie" (1909), Florian Maria or "Marie" (1911), Constantine, who died at birth (1912), Felicitas or "Flitz" (1913), Francis or "Frank" (1915), Alberta or "Berty" (1917), Paul (1918). [8]

During the Great Depression the majority of Americans experienced great hardships, but the Dreiling family would have been considered "poor" by even the average American of that time. With 19 mouths to feed, meat was a rarity unless someone shot a jackrabbit. The Dreiling family lived off the land and made due with what they had. Many of the children would later experience intestinal problems, which Kilian attributed to their poor, potato-heavy diet. However, the Dreilings possessed in abundance, the quality Jesus referred to as "poor in spirit." [5]

The Dreiling family was very active in their parish community and like many of their neighbors, unable to contribute much financially, donated seven wagonloads of stone to build the new St. Fidelis Church in Victoria, KS in 1911. So beautiful was the sight of this church that none other than William Jennings Bryan nicknamed it the "Cathedral of the Plains."[6] At its completion, it had a seating capacity of 1,100 and was then, the largest church west of the Mississippi. This beautiful cathedral stands today as a testament to the faith of the early Volga-German settlers. Many of the stained glass windows of the cathedral bear the names of some of the most prominent families of the community, including the Dreiling family.

Like most Americans growing up in this period, Kilian learned to be extremely resourceful. This quality would later prove extremely useful during his years as a chaplain and a pastor. He also developed an appreciation for the "little things" that made life beautiful. Kilian's family taught him to see God in everyday life. Surrounded by a large, boisterous, loving family he learned to live life fully and completely. Growing up with 16 siblings exposed Kilian to constant social interaction. This helped him develop an ability to identify with and relate to people, especially children. He also became adept at developing strong arguments in support of his beliefs.

Kilian watched three of his brothers leave home to serve in the U.S. Army during WWI. This brought a great deal of pain to his parents. Daily family prayers were offered for their safe return and in the case of all three, these prayers were answered. Kilian was too young to be drafted, but he vividly remembered the war stories that his brothers told upon their return. These experiences helped instill a strong patriotism in Kilian at an early age. The Dreiling family also had more reasons to appreciate the freedom and democracy they experienced in America. They had fled a totalitarian regime in Russia, and would later hear firsthand horror stories of the brutal and repressive Bolshevik regime from relatives in Soviet Russia. [5]

Fr. Kilian's mother was a strong influence throughout his life. A strong-willed woman, she also possessed a keen sense of humor. Family friends describe the Dreiling home as full of laughter. Fr. Kilian would later fondly recall some of his mother's sayings.

"We must love our neighbor, but that doesn't mean we must have coffee with them." Agnes apparently wanted her children to understand that there were different degrees of love and friendship. "As the horse goes, the buggy goes. If you think right you will act right." [7]

She was a firm believer in the futility of fighting against human nature. She would say, "You can throw human nature out the front door and it will run around the house and come back in through the back door. Or, you can throw human nature out the back door and it will run around the house and enter through the front door. If you throw half out the back door and half out the front door, it will run half way around the house and come in the window."[7]

Agnes's blend of humor and quick wit with wisdom, became character traits of many of her children, with Kilian being one of the best examples. Later in life, one of her older sons suggested that he bring his new bride home to live with him and his mother. (This was long after Kilian's father Michael Dreiling had passed away). His mother's response was, "Son, even a sparrow knows better than that. See that hill yonder? Build a house on it and I will pay for it. Far better we separate as friends than live together as enemies."[7]

Mrs. Barbara Goffena, who came to know Fr. Kilian late in his life, described the impact that Agnes Dreiling had on Fr. Kilian.

"Fr. Dreiling always spoke highly of his dear mother, who played a very important part in his life. Being brought up during some very hard times, she taught him to be generous with what little they had. And a generous man he was. He couldn't cook a meal, which he thoroughly enjoyed, without giving most of it away. How many times he gave me a dish of food to take home and later when he came to visit at our house he never came empty-handed. Whatever you did for him he did twice as much for you."

Fr. Kilian's decision to enter the seminary at the tender age of 14 was strongly influenced by his mother. She supported his decision and was proud to have her son study for the priesthood. Religious vocations were not uncommon in the Dreiling family. Kilian's own sister Verginta also chose the vocation of a Catholic nun, and two of his cousins and a nephew followed him into the seminary. In any case, his mother Agnes certainly would not have been able to afford to send him to college. Fr. Leo, the local Catholic priest also played a role in helping Kilian select the priesthood. Later, when Fr. Kilian decided to become an army chaplain, he would first seek the permission of his mother. Such a tender gesture of respect and compassion provides us an indication of how much Fr. Kilian loved and revered his mother.

Another factor that might have hastened Kilian's decision to leave the family farm for the seminary, was the untimely death of his father. Some time before this, Michael Dreiling had suffered a nervous breakdown. The stresses of raising 17 children during the depression in a first generation immigrant family might have done the same to many others. Now, Agnes had to face this daunting task alone.

Kilian's departure would mean one less mouth to feed, and he must have certainly been aware of this fact as he departed for the Precious Blood Seminary in Carthagena, Ohio. He would now be alone, over 1000 miles from the only family and friends he knew.

Chapter 3

The young seminarian

Fr. Kilian would later say of his decision to enter the priesthood, that he chose his vocation in a similar fashion to how many of us would choose a spouse. That is to say, Fr. Kilian carefully considered that this would be a lifetime commitment that once made, would require the surrendering of his entire heart and soul.

In any case, this was a tremendous act of faith for Kilian. He must certainly have had fears about leaving home, yet he was willing to face them. Entering a seminary over 1000 miles from home was also a demonstration of how much Kilian loved Jesus, and of his willingness to place himself in the hands of our Lord. Yet it reveals another side of Fr. Kilian that would later become more evident: his love of adventure.

The order that young Kilian joined was The Society of the Precious Blood of Jesus (C.PP.S.), introduced into the United States by Fr. Francis de Sales Brunner. Fr. Brunner had come from Switzerland in 1844 with seven priests and brothers to work with the German immigrants in Northwest Ohio. The Society was founded by St. Gaspar del Bufalo, a Roman priest in 1815, in obedience to Pope Pius VII's call for a renewed emphasis on "parish mission work." [1] Far from home, 14-year-old Kilian felt some reassurance in being able to converse in the native language of his parents.

When young Kilian arrived at the seminary on September 9, 1924, he did not own a single pair of shoes.[2] He must have looked like a pretty raw recruit. At first, Kilian was assigned to St. Mary's novitiate, a preparatory school. Later, he would move to St. Charles seminary at Carthagena for formal instruction. The priests there would soon discover that young Kilian Dreiling also had a great deal of raw talent and native intelligence. This talent, when combined with Kilian's deep faith and his passion for saving souls, would produce an inspirational leader with boundless energy.

None of this however, was easy for Kilian. In fact, he would later recount the difficulties he incurred because of his problems with the English language. It was necessary for Kilian to work harder than most of his classmates because he had to translate all of his lessons first from English into German, and then into Latin. Fr. Kilian would later look back on his years at Carthagena with great fondness. Here he grew from a boy to a man, and he would establish deep friendships that would last a lifetime.

Fr. Kilian also developed his powerful speaking skills at Carthagena, and became a strong defender of his Catholic faith. He also demonstrated unusual wisdom at an early age. When another seminarian confided in Fr. Kilian that he secretly wished he could be as good at public speaking as Kilian, Kilian responded, "See the different kind of trees? Have you ever heard the apple tree complain that it could not produce peaches, or the peach tree complain that it could not produce pears? Why complain that you cannot preach as well as I can? Why not face the fact that God deliberately, willfully, from all eternity decreed and ordained that each and every one of us has a certain talent and a certain weakness. Let us concentrate and develop, specialize in these talents and not envy anyone who has other talents. To accept ourselves with our weaknesses and our talents is to say 'Amen' to the infinite wisdom of knowledge of Almighty God." [3]

One story told about Fr. Kilian from his seminary days attests to his love of cooking good food. From his German mother, Kilian learned the art of cooking, as well as the joys of sharing the fruits of his labor with friends. When his fellow seminarians played a joke on Kilian by substituting plaster of paris for flour, the resulting pound cake had the texture of a smooth brick. After Kilian threw the "cake" in the garbage, it kept showing up back in his room. Finally, Kilian went outside to an unknown spot and buried it. Many years later, during an excavation on the seminary grounds, some very puzzled construction workers unearthed Kilian's "cake." [4]

The following story is told in Fr. Kilian's own words. It describes an event at Kilian's commencement Mass that made an indelible impression upon him. It is also an indication of how much love and respect Kilian and his fellow seminarians had for the priests who were their teachers, mentors and spiritual advisors during these critical and formative years.

Pre-Vatican II

In the early and mid-thirties, we had woefully few retired priests at St. Charles Seminary. However, if we lacked in quantity we were blessed with quality. One such member was Fr. Paulinus Trost, the crusty old octogenarian. Fr. Trost had few likes but many dislikes. The student body was, fortunately, one of his likes — provided they did not whistle in the corridors. But top priority was given to his loyal and faithful companion — his cane. It was his sacred cow. With it he managed to walk the halls with security and agility. But far more importantly, he employed it for many other reasons. With it, he stomped the floor to emphasize a point, get the attention of a passerby, and it was not unknown that he even vigorously poked the chest of a passerby to divert his attention. We, the students loved the cantankerous old painter not in spite of his idiosyncrasies, but because of them.

And so it happened that we, the deacons, dared to approach Fr. Knapke, our rector, with this request. "Would it be possible that Fr. Paulinus would be the celebrant and preach for the feast of the Immaculate Conception, perhaps for the last time, December 8th?"

Fr. Knapke rubbed his nose mightily and finally said, "Boys, boys, he won't do it, he won't do it." We countered, "But Father, if you tell him that we, the student body asked for that favor???" Again Fr. Knapke belabored his nose and said, "I will try, but he won't do it."

Weeks passed and not a peep. The cause was closed; we thought. But came Dec. 7th, Fr. Knapke banged the bell heftily and with a grin announced in no uncertain voice, "Mass tomorrow at 10:00 and Fr. Paulinus will be the honored celebrant and homilist." The applause that followed shattered the "silentium altum" all the way to Siberia and back.

Mark, my cousin, and I were subdeacon and deacon respectively. With infinite care we led the honored guest celebrant to the steps of the altar; rejoiced exceedingly when he belted out the penitential psalm in clear, loud Latin, and gave it additional emphasis by stomping his cane recklessly. Only once was the situation shattered — a deacon in the stalls thought out loud, "That poor mouse between two elephants."

Confident now that all would go well, we literally hoisted Fr. Paulinus up the three steps to intone the Gloria. That, indeed, he did with profound vigor. All went well...until the time for the sermon. With intense Unction Father professed his theme clearly but not quite sinlessly. In an effort to make amends, he floundered even more miserably. With bitter determination, he tried once more, only to find himself clogged in an irresistable dead center. His mental blackout was as total as the devil's soul. He looked longingly to the students, next to the sisters, to the brothers, but help came from nowhere. No, not even his best friend, his faithful cane, could extricate him from this disgrace. The terrible crisis came to a head when poor Father simply did what any child of God would do. He wept openly and humbly "in conspectu omnium." Eventually, (which seemed to us a century), he composed himself, apologetically turned to the sisters' choir, then to the nave, the students' area, then to the brothers to the right, and in his own German dialect he said quiveringly, "Sisters, students and brothers, I guess I am just not worthy to speak about so noble a person as the Mother of Jesus." With that he turned about face, intoned the Credo, finished the Mass without another flaw, yes, even with a flourish.

As we led him back to the sacristy, the cane still stomping the floor, even more vigorously, he repeated over and over as he looked from side to side, "Mea Culpa, Mea Culpa, Mea Maxima Culpa."

This time it was the entire community that wept silently. Then, and even today, for all who recall this historic event, it is commonly repeated, "The best sermon ever preached at St. Charles." "O Felix Culpa!"

During the summer preceding Kilian's final year as a seminarian at St. Charles he, along with four other seminarians including his cousin Marcellus Dreiling, was inspired to build a small shrine to the Blessed

Mother on the seminary grounds. Tired of seeing a large Pieta gathering dust in its unseemly location adjacent to the basketball floor, the bold young men decided to take matters into their own hands. Without asking for anyone's permission, a "horrible dictu" [5] in the days of strict observance, they selected a site adjacent to a small lake, and began construction.

Despite the fact that none of them knew anything about construction, the little stone structure was sound, and still stands today as a testament to the faith of the five seminarians. Perhaps because of its "unauthorized" beginnings, the "Shrine by the Little Lake," as it is known today, never received official recognition by the C.PP.S. until 2001, when Rector Fr. James Seibert officiated over its solemn blessing and dedication. Nevertheless, the seminarians were quite proud and satisfied with the results of their labors. As Fr. Hugh Uhrich, one of the five "conspirators" later stated, "On the day that the large Pieta was put in place in the 'Little Lake Shrine,' we were happy...Mary's statue had found a home." [5]

Fr. Kilian would return to Carthagena many times throughout his life. He would spend his final years in retirement there, walking the same hallways he walked as a young seminarian and sharing a lifetime of beautiful stories with his fellow priests. Another resident priest would later comment, "Only the barns here are older than Fr. Kilian." [6] Kilian would eventually outlive almost all of the friends he made as a seminarian at Carthagena.

Chapter 4
A License to Save Souls

After ordination on May 10th, 1936, 28 year old Fr. Kilian Dreiling was assigned to Brunnerdale Seminary in Canton, OH as a professor.[1] This was a position of some responsibility for a newly ordained priest, and Kilian's first assignment provides early evidence that his superiors in the C.PP.S. order had high expectations for him.

Fifteen months later, in September of 1937, Fr. Kilian was assigned to be the Assistant Pastor at Holy Trinity Church in St. Matthews, KY, a Louisville suburb. Here Fr. Kilian would face his first major crisis as a priest.

Fr. Kilian had only been at Holy Trinity for a few weeks when their beautiful new church burned down. Shortly thereafter, Fr. Bartholomew Besinger, the pastor, had a heart attack. Any hopes Fr. Kilian had of "easing" into pastoral life went up in flames along with Holy Trinity. Fr. Kilian now faced a major crisis. His parishioners were devastated, not only by the loss of their beautiful structure made possible by their own sacrifices, but they were without their beloved pastor as well. In speaking of Fr. Bart, Kilian would later say, "A greater man God never made."

Fr. Kilian rose to his first major challenge with a speed and energy that amazed the stunned parishioners of Holy Trinity. He quickly arranged for an improvised Mass schedule to be held in the gymnasium and energized the community by beginning construction on a new Holy Trinity church building. Fr. Kilian also solicited and received assistance from local Protestant churches, an early indication of his ecumenical attitudes.

One of the young parishioners, Elsie Schneider, gives a vivid recollection of the young Fr. Kilian. "My father and I met Fr. Kilian within the first two weeks of his arrival, and that turned out to be the beginning of a lifelong friendship with our family. He was like a brother to all of us. We loved him dearly. We always knew the feeling was mutual. Our parish survived and flourished under the leadership and guidance of Father Kilian." [2]

After a short 14 months, Fr. Kilian was assigned to the "mission band." This was a different role, but one that underscored the principles upon which the Precious Blood Society was founded. Essentially, mission priests lived in "Mission Houses," which were usually average-looking single family homes occupied by several priests. The priests would travel extensively within their assigned regions giving spiritual revivals or "missions." Fr. Kilian's pre-WWII missionary assignments would see him stationed at Mission Houses in Charlottesville, VA, new Cumberland, PA and finally, Cleveland, OH. [1]

It was during this period from October of 1938 until June of 1943 that Fr. Kilian would develop and perfect his oratorical skills. Mission work is not for the feint of heart. By its definition, it requires a priest with fire and passion. He must engage his audience quickly, motivate and inspire them, and then move on. A significant objective of the mission was to inspire the parishioners to come to the confessional. Fr. Joseph Marling, Provincial of the C.PP.S. during the war years wrote about this subject.

"It may be more gratifying to see the church crowded each night but the success of the mission does not depend upon the crowds. Surely we want people there to listen to the sermons and instructions, but the real good is done in the confessional. The words of St. Alphonsus still hold true: 'If the only good accruing from missions would be the rectifying of invalid and sacrilegious confessions, that would be ample justification for having them.'" [3]

Fr. Kilian left us with a vivid account of what mission work was like.

"I gave a mission in Detroit once. We were there for three solid weeks. We heard confessions early in the morning, before noon, in the afternoon and preeminently at night after the big sermon. After three weeks I was tired, dreadfully tired and after the close, at 2:00 in the afternoon, I crossed the lawn, the shortest distance between two points. I reached the knob of the rectory, thinking of going to bed and resting. Just as I reached for the knob a man came running across the lawn and he pleaded with me, 'Father, will you hear my confession?'

"I said, 'My good man, I heard confessions for three solid weeks, morning, before noon, in the afternoon and later at night. Why didn't you come then?'

"He stammered and he stuttered and finally he broke down and cried. He said, 'Father, seven times, seven times I stood outside your confessional. I never had the courage to go in until now.'

"I took him by the arm and said, 'My good man, let's go back to church.'

"I went back into the confessional at 10 minutes until 3:00, and 10 minutes till 7:00 I was still there. I asked each and every penitent, for the simple reason of learning, 'Why didn't you come during the mission?' and each and every time the answer was the same. 'Until now I never had the courage; I never had the grace; I never had the "manliness" until now.'

"It taught me vigorously and forcefully, two important things. The first is, never be too harsh to a penitent in the confessional. I asked a penitent one time, 'Are you really and truly sincere in your confession?' You know what he said to me? 'Father, if you only knew how long it took me to gather, to muster the courage to come in here and to confess, you would never have asked that question.' I never did after that. Therefore, this lesson taught me to be kind, to be merciful, in other words to be exactly as our Lord would have been.

"Secondly, there is a tremendous amount of grace that God pours into the souls of people during an exercise, during a mission, retreat or a day of recollection. If only we would acknowledge it. If only we would be thankful for it. If only we would really and truly and sincerely be conscious of it." [4]

Apparently, long hours were the norm rather than the exception for the missionary. However, it is also apparent that Fr. Kilian found this work to be very rewarding. He would prove to be an excellent missionary and this experience would prepare him well for the most demanding assignment of his life; That of an army chaplain in WWII. Fr. Kilian's talent for instilling the courage necessary to bring the penitent to the confessional would soon be put to good use in the Pacific Theatre.

A young Killian Dreiling (2nd from right) poses with his four older brothers, three of whom fought in the U.S. Army during WWI.

St. Fidelis Church, the "Cathedral of the Plains" stands as a testament to the faith of the early Russian or "Volga-German" settlers in Victoria, Kansas. Fr. Kilian Dreiling's family donated 7 wagonloads of stone as their contribution to its construction (1908–11)

A young Fr. Kilian Dreiling during his pre-war, missionary years during a visit home to Kansas.

A handsome, 28 year-old Fr. Kilian Dreiling as he appeared in May, 1936 upon ordination. In his first assignment he would serve as a professor at Brunnerale seminary in Canton, Ohio.

St. Charles Seminary, the Motherhouse of the Cincinnati Province of the Missionaries of the Precious Blood (C.PP.S.) in Carthagena, Ohio. Fr. Francis de Sales Brunner came from Switzerland in 1844 with seven priests to minister to the German immigrants who had settled in Northwest Ohio.

The official seal of the C.PP.S. with the Paschal Lamb as the central theme.

Today, the symbol most often seen representing the C.PP.S. is the Cup and Cross.

Missonaries of the Precious Blood (C.PP.S.)
Founded in 1815 by St. Gaspar del Bufalo the society was formed for the purpose of preaching missions to invigorate a church which had grown weak under the reign of Napoleon.

Chapter 5

A New Calling

In retrospect, it is not surprising that Fr. Kilian Dreiling would volunteer to serve his parents' adopted country as well as his church. Fr. Kilian was after all, a great patriot. Few Americans appreciated the freedoms afforded to U.S. citizens more than the Dreiling family. They had fled religious and cultural persecution in Russia, and their relatives had been murdered and "scattered to the winds" by the communist regimes of both Lenin and Stalin.

Furthermore, three of Fr. Kilian's older brothers had taken up arms in defense of these freedoms during WWI. All returned with a much greater understanding and appreciation of the word, "freedom." No doubt Kilian heard many first-hand accounts of the bravery and sacrifice exhibited by the American soldiers fighting in France. He was riveted by one story in particular. This story would be forever linked with a song, which became very special to Fr. Kilian. He would later research and write the following article about this wonderful song, and how its author Catherine Lee Bates became inspired to write it after a trip to the American West. This trip included visits to Pike's Peak and the 1893 Chicago world's fair with its "alabaster buildings."

"Alone in her hotel room after her visit to Pike's Peak, she hurriedly scribbled her inner-most sentiments about her country and its people on a piece of scrap paper. However, the poem was never published until 1895. She piously kept it under cover out of sheer modesty. Once published, no restraint however forceful, could fence it in. It took to wings with the force of a hurricane. Countries adopted it body and soul with only a slight change: Canada! Canada! For America! America! Mexico mi Mexico! Etc. It was shortly sung in church and halls, on streets and sports fields, during civic and religious celebrations. Bates remained almost childishly modest about her glorious masterpiece. Only once did she give expression to her pride in her now famous work.

"It was November 11, 1918, the day the guns fell silent when the air in and around Verdun, France cleared and peace unexpectedly permeated the sky... was surrender day. It was Armistice day.

"American soldiers deserted their soggy trenches, scaled a knoll and spontaneously intoned, with greatest reverence and emotion, the beloved hymn 'America the Beautiful.' Soon soldiers of other nations deserted water-drenched trenches, surrounded the Americans and lustily joined the universally sacred love song. With tears streaming down their faces the chorus took on momentum. It raged with sympathy and joy and gratitude, forgiveness, it spoke the language of Americans and by adoption, the language of every other friendly nation. It spoke firmly of a unique people, back to the same people in a holy and unforgettable psalm of gratitude.

"As I researched this paper, a rumbling rose from the epicenter of my soul. Over and over I searched for the clue, but only when I came to the song on the knoll did it surface. My brother Ray, one of three in the 1st WW, was in Verdun France on that very same day, indeed, he was in the very same soggy trenches, he joined in the very same song, he joined in the very same mutual tears and gratitude. Over and over we, his little brothers and sister, listened with baited breath as he recalled for us the war, but especially and most often, the Day of Surrender-Armistice Day. That he told best and we remembered even better."

After December 7, 1941, the sons of the veterans of the First World War were called upon to defend these freedoms as well. Like their fathers before them, they volunteered by the hundreds of thousands.

After witnessing so many young American boys go off to war, Fr. Kilian began to question his mission. His order, the C.PP.S., would eventually send 45 priests to serve with distinction in the U.S. armed forces during WWII. This was a disproportionately large percentage for an order with only 307 ordained priests.[1] Fr. Kilian became acutely aware of the need for chaplains to minister to the needs of American soldiers far from home. Many of the C.PP.S. priests had already asked for and received permission to serve with the armed forces in this capacity.

Fr. Robert Conway describes what Fr. Dreiling told some young seminarians about his decision to enlist in the Army as a chaplain.

"Before entering military service he told us that he wanted to enter to prevent, as he said, the returning soldiers from 'becoming radicals.' I guess he was thinking of the chaos in Germany and Russia after WWI."

Before Fr. Kilian could go however, he sought the blessing of his dear mother. This was a beautiful act of respect and admiration for Fr. Kilian, indicating just how much he loved and revered his mother. After having three sons serve in WWI, Agnes Dreiling had every right to feel she had fulfilled her obligations to her adopted country. She was not happy about Fr. Kilian's decision. Fr. Kilian however, knew his mother well, and he knew just how to appeal to her maternal instincts. Fr. Kilian tells the following beautiful story in a sermon he gave many years later to his former Army brethren about the special love that exists only between a mother and her child.

"What I have to say about my Mother, you, each and every one of you could duplicate a thousand times over, with emphasis and equal pride in speaking of your own, kind mothers. When I definitely decided to join the service, I felt filially obligated, even though I was well past eighteen and a man of the cloth for seven years, to consult my Mother and secure her kind approval. Keenly conscious that she had given three sons to the First World War, I gingerly approached her and fearfully stated my solemn intent. The reaction was prompt and excruciatingly brutal. She covered her face and broke into the bitterest kind of weeping. I can never recall a pain so sharp, so keen and so cruel, as the pain I so thoughtlessly inflicted on this kindly creature, my Mother. Much later she controlled her feelings of resentment or Motherly hurt and finally said, 'Child, I gave three sons to the First World War, and even now, from morning to night, word may come that your brother, my youngest, may have gone down over Europe in his B-17. Must I sacrifice still more? Would you add even more to my sorrow and anxiety?'

"It was only because I inherited, and in great measure, strength and steel from this, yet stronger and more courageous woman, my Mother, that I managed to speak even more boldly. 'But Mother' I said, 'if your youngest were in need of spiritual help would you not hope, and even pray, that someone would attend to his spiritual needs?'

"I watched intently, scrupulously, and may I add fearfully, as she made her next painful move. Make it she did! She verbalized her feelings, her determination, her painful conclusion, not only in speech, but in physical transfiguration. Her face hardened like marble, her posture became erect, and suddenly, I thought she stood ten feet taller than the Statue of Liberty. Resolutely, articulately, almost brutally she spoke: more correctly, commanded, 'Child' she said, 'go...join...you may well be too late to help your brother, but every son whom you help will be as dear to his mother as you and my youngest are to me. Be brave, son. Go and God be with you.' Only much later did I actually learn what an appalling price she paid in my going to the service."

With these prophetic words from his mother echoing in his ear, Fr. Kilian joined the U.S. Army as a chaplain.

The first step for any clergyman aspiring to become a chaplain in the U.S. armed forces is basic training. This is necessary to weed out the "faint of heart." Before a chaplain can be in a position to offer encouragement and strength to others, he must first demonstrate that he is physically and mentally tough enough to become a soldier. One of Fr. Kilian's C.PP.S. colleagues, Fr. Edward Moorman, even joined the famous 101st Airborne Division, jumping into enemy territory alongside his fellow soldiers. [2]

Another C.PP.S. chaplain, Fr. Karl Wuest, gives us this description of basic training in July of 1942 at Fort Benjamin Harrison in Indianapolis, IN. [3]

"Perhaps you will find our order of day interesting. We rise at 5:45. Calisthenics and hike, 6:00-6:30. Mass at 6:30 and breakfast at 7:00. At 8:00 we priests say the rosary in common. Then classes from 8:30 until noon, an hour of which is close order drill. Lunch, and then classes from 1;00 to5:30, including another drill from 7:00 to 9:00. It's a full day. Living in a dormitory is strange. Our belongings are stored in a wall locker and trunk. Inspection of bed and locker takes place every morning, and it isn't a casual thing at all. One will be torn apart, and orders given for its remaking. Personal inspection, every Saturday."

Fr. Karl Wuest would later witness a great deal of horrific fighting with General Mark Clark's Fifth U.S. Army in Italy. Fr. Wuest would also distinguish himself for bravery and would be the recipient of a commendation bearing the signature of General Clark. [4]

Chapter 6

Off to War

Upon being commissioned a U.S. Army officer, Fr. Kilian was sent to the South Pacific where he served briefly with the 376th infantry, 94th Division and the 1112 combat engineers. Fr. Kilian's next assignment with the 239th combat engineers lasted a bit longer. [1] During the months that he was assigned to the engineers however, he was able to leave a lasting impression.

One young serviceman from the 239th Lou Weisgerber recalls his first meeting with Fr. Kilian upon the young priest's arrival.

"It was late in 1943 when I first met Fr. Dreiling. The location was Camp Forest, TN, just prior to boarding the troop train to San Francisco. The battalion was billeted in 'tent city.' It was a cold, rainy day in Tennessee. I returned to the operations tent to find the sergeant talking to a new Second Lieutenant, just assigned to the battalion. He introduced him as the 'new chaplain Fr. Dreiling.' I stuck out my hand to shake hands with him and he looked at me and said, 'boy do I have my work cut out for me here.' " [2]

From San Francisco, the 239th Engineers embarked upon a 28-day voyage on the Dutch freighter, "Kota Agoeing," to the South Pacific. Aboard the freighter, Mr. Weisgerber adds an illuminating story about how Fr. Kilian was able to very quickly command the respect of his new unit, while instilling the confidence that comes from being in the presence of a strong, spiritual leader.

"Near the end of our voyage, Fr. Dreiling decided to hold mini-conferences with a group of about four or five Catholic sergeants. Most of the time was spent on telling us that though we were raised Catholic, and should not take the life of another, this was war and we should not hesitate to shoot the enemy if the situation presented itself. We were not committing any sin by killing in a war.

He then proceeded to tell us that we were also relieved of all fasting and abstinence. The Jewish boys could eat ham and pork and we could eat meat on Fridays. One sergeant spoke up and said that he didn't observe the 'no meat on Friday law' anyway when he was at home. He ate meat when he felt like it. There was a short pause, then a long emphasized discussion on the (importance of) observance of church laws when we were supposed to. Needless to say, that sergeant never made any other statements regarding the rules of the church when Fr. Dreiling was around." [2]

Early in 1944, Fr. Kilian's first chapel in the South Pacific was built on "Goodenough Island." The local natives utilized local materials with logs for pews and a thatched roof. Weisgerber recalls it as a "beautiful little chapel." Fr. Kilian fondly describes this event in a letter sent to his superiors back in Carthagena, OH. He also describes the increased religious response from the men, perhaps adding fuel to the argument that the religious fervor of the soldier increases the closer he is to combat. Fr. Kilian also speaks of an unpleasant encounter with another chaplain, evidence that not all units were fortunate enough to have a spiritual minister of Fr. Kilian's caliber.

"We are working on two chapels which will soon be in fine shape. It is the first time I enjoy a chapel since I am in the Army. They have thatched roofs, open sides and doors- like the caves: open to man and beast. After benediction the other night, the men were so happy that they decided to plant small coconut trees all around the chapel. My Protestant co-worker is not much interested. He spends his time playing bridge.

"Religion has taken on a new and decided emphasis. It is hard to believe the men could change so much. The law of Eucharistic Feast has been entirely recalled and the communions and confessions have increased remarkably. There is an average of four hundred Communions a Sunday. On Sunday I say three masses. At the first Mass last Sunday the attendance was 275. Of these only 200 could get into the chapel and the rest stood outside looking through imaginary windows. The second Mass was 17 miles away, and about the same number attended, but the chapel is larger and all got inside.

The third was near the sea, with 175 present. It is impossible to hear half the confessions, hence we grant General Absolution (to) all (attending) the masses. The roads are strictly primitive. There are about ten streams to cross on my trips. So far, I have always succeeded in getting across, thanks to the American jeep. There is nothing so determined as the jeep... often the water sweeps over both seats.

"On the way over I had some difficulty with a Chaplain who boasted that he hated Catholics. I informed him that I would report him as soon as we reached port. He suddenly changed colors, but I kept my word. My Colonel insisted that I do so. We gain nothing by tolerating breeches like that." [3]

Shortly before the 239th left Goodenough Island, Fr. Kilian asked Sgt. Lou Weisgerber to come and see him. Weisgerber was thinking that he might have done something wrong, but was surprised to find out from Fr. Kilian that the 239th's chaplain was being reassigned to the 92nd Evacuation Hospital. [2] It was with this distinguished unit that Fr. Kilian was to spend the balance of the war, and he would become its heart and soul.

However, Fr. Kilian would always have a special place in his heart for the boys in his first unit, the 239th Combat Engineers. Many years after the war, he would be the catalyst for their annual reunions and he kept in touch with many of the 239th's soldiers until his death at the age of 90.

Chapter 7

Hollandia, the First Invasion

By all historical accounts, the invasion of Hollandia, on the northern coast of New Guinea was a complete success for General MacArthur's U.S. Army forces. Through a series of brilliant feints, and with the help of solid intelligence by U.S. reconnaissance forces and Australian Coast Watchers, MacArthur was able to take the Japanese completely by surprise. Consequently, the entire invasion force landed nearly unopposed. Japanese forces, expecting an invasion elsewhere, had vacated their defensive positions only days before. [1]

To the soldiers' complete surprise, General MacArthur himself was spotted wading ashore among the GIs. MacArthur would later call this invasion, "the most brilliantly executed operation I have ever witnessed." Total American casualties were 28 dead and 95 wounded. [1]

Fr. Kilian gives this detailed, first-hand account of the Hollandia landings in a letter sent to the C.PP.S. Fathers back in Carthagena, OH. In speaking about his first priestly duties in a combat situation, his concern for the soldiers or "boys" is evident.

"Thank God! The invasion is over. It was only a few days, but while it lasted it was a tremendous spectacle. Sailing along in the blackness of the night, sleeping on deck, one had to keep one eye open as it were, for the alert, announcing enemy air raids. It is not difficult to pray in such circumstances. At the sound of the alert, the ship was pitch dark, and not a sound was heard aboard ship. In the moonlight it was possible at times to discern the outline of some of the ships that constituted the convoy, moving along silently, slowly, majestically. It all seemed so innocent, so peaceful, so harmless. Overhead however, the men on lookout were tense with anxiety, searching the sky in every direction, quietly moving guns into position, silently signaling to one another in secret code. Huge warships, protecting the convoy, would circle in and out among the transport ships more rapidly than before. There were plenty of them, but I did not learn the full number until after we had landed. The invasion as you know, was a complete success. What we thought would require twelve days took only four. The Japs had retreated some days before we landed, and within a short time we had the three air strips, 280 planes, row upon row of trucks, tanks, bulldozers and equipment of every kind. It remains only to clean up. Some lives undoubtedly will be taken, but the loss up to now has been practically nil. When General McArthur reported that this campaign was a complete success, he was giving the American people the absolute truth.

"Yesterday was Sunday. I had four Masses, and I have been worried about it since. I had the three scheduled Masses, and then learned that a battalion was holding a line at the left flank, up in the mountains. I went up there and those boys wanted Mass. So I heard Confessions and offered Mass in a gully between the mountains, where man had never before set foot. The non-Catholic boys also asked for services, so I preached a sermon on the act of Perfect Contrition. My jeep stands on the mountainside, next to my tent. Here I have Mass every night, and the boys come from all around. The jeep has not moved from the position since I first placed it there. The roads are terrible. In some places logs are piled as high as seven feet deep, and still they go down and down. The engineers are building a road over the mountain. I have been with the men so much that the Commanding Officer objected that I was holding up the project. When the job is finished our engineers should find their work extolled in the American newspapers. Air raids have now practically ceased, and soon we shall be as safe as we were in the other area. Now I shall attempt to bring some food, cigarettes and toilet articles to the men in the field. Remember me to all...It will be a holiday when I receive a letter." [2]

This letter gives some indication of the energy level and dedication that Fr. Kilian brought to his role as chaplain. He would do anything in his power to help his "boys." Fr. Kilian was known to sleep on average, 4 hours a night. As one officer later recalled, "when the Padre slept, no one knew." [3]

Two units that were part of the invasion fleet at Hollandia were the 239th Engineers and the 92nd Evacuation hospital. It was after this invasion that Fr. Kilian was reassigned from the 239th to the 92nd. One of the officers from the 92nd had high praise for the Army Engineers at this time. Capt. E.F. Pfile was quoted in a U.S. newspaper saying, "It is marvelous what the engineers do. They built more roads in two days than the Japs did in two years." [1]

At Hollandia, the U.S. Army also liberated a group of around 100 German Catholic missionary priests, who were extremely happy to see the Americans. This was also the first time they would hear first-hand accounts of Japanese atrocities. One German priest told of witnessing two captured American airmen who were starved, and then beheaded. [1] Fr. Kilian's German language skills were almost certainly of great value in this situation. The 92nd would encounter many such missionaries, and Fr. Kilian always went to great lengths to look after their needs.

Due to their proximity to the combat, the 92nd Evacuation Hospital was not exempt from enemy fire or bombings from the air. On the first night in Hollandia, a lone Japanese medium or "Betty" bomber dropped a lucky bomb near a spot where some ammunition had been quickly stored. This began a series of chain reaction explosions up and down the beach, also destroying the food stores. The men quickly improvised by eating captured Japanese rations including rice, fish and Sake. [4]

The explosions were finally brought to an end by the bravery of a young Texan who had volunteered to try to force a gap in the stacked line of bombs with a bulldozer. Once, a bomb destroyed the blade on the front of his bulldozer and the Texan, unshaken, simply said, "Get me another CAT." The GI was not entirely selfless however. He had volunteered only after a 30-day furlough had been promised to anyone who could end the carnage. [4] This type of common heroism, often laced with humor would earn the American GI's Fr. Kilian Dreiling's undying respect. He would later say, "The American GI does not have to wait for orders, he knows what to do." [4]

It was with the 92nd Evacuation Hospital that Fr. Kilian would experience his most trying and harrowing moments of the war. Fr.

Kilian's time with the 92nd was also the period from which he drew the majority of his powerful wartime stories. Most of these stories are included in the pages ahead. Hollandia was the first of many South Pacific invasion beaches they would encounter together. The 92nd would arrive on D-Day + 1, and begin taking care of the wounded and dying soldiers. This allowed Fr. Kilian to minister not only to the soldiers of his own outfit, but to thousands of scared, wounded and dying soldiers as well. This experience would profoundly change and shape Fr. Kilian's life, as well as the lives of those around him.

Chapter 8

The 92nd Evacuation Hospital

Before moving on to the other Pacific campaigns, a little background on the 92nd Evacuation Hospital will help explain this unit's role in these campaigns, and provide useful background for Fr. Kilian's upcoming stories.

The 92nd was a forerunner of what would later become more popularly known as "M.A.S.H. units." Evacuation Hospitals were designed to be mobile hospitals, able to pick up everything at a moment's notice and re-deploy in one day. This they did in remarkable fashion. The unit had a complement of 255 officers and enlisted men. "We were supposed to have only 500 patients," Fr. Kilian would later say. "Usually, we had 1,000, and not infrequently, 1,500." [1]

Many of the 40 doctors and 40 nurses from the 92nd had been recruited from Colorado, and some of their wartime antics were reminiscent of scripts from the 70's TV show "M.A.S.H." The medical staff was supported by a detachment of soldiers who had been trained in the Mojave Desert, and were originally intended to be sent to North Africa. These men served as truck drivers and mechanics, cooks, logistical and supply personnel and administrative staff. "Ward men" were also assigned supplemental nursing duties. Men who didn't have any special skills were commonly referred to as "yard-birds." Often, the 92nd was so close to the front lines that they had to man their own perimeter defense, a good job for a yardbird.

Before being sent to the fighting in New Guinea, the 92nd traveled on a converted luxury liner, the "Lurline" to Brisbane, Australia, and then on to Rockhampton. There they stayed for several months, training for the invasions which would soon follow, and enjoying the hospitality of the grateful Australian people. My father described to me how the Australian women enjoyed the company of the American soldiers, who they thought acted and sounded like cowboys.

The antics of three doctors in particular became legendary within the 92nd. A retrospective, provided by the supply officer Lt. Ed Gray 44 years after the war with tongue planted firmly in cheek, recalls one of their more memorable incidents.

"Bill Baker, Ray 'Baldy' Nethery and John 'Black Jack' Mihalic spent most of their working time repairing broken bodies and their spare time raising Caine. At Rockhampton club, their most famous venture was at the local officers' club where Baldy, a bit into his cups and in an aggressive mood, offered his chin to an MP Captain and requested a hit. The Captain obliged and Baldy went 'arse over teakettle' into the bar. There was quite a ruckus and the three of them were escorted, none too gently, by an MP detachment to our camp, where they spent several hours nursing their bruised egos while making great plans for vengeance.

"Late that night, Sgt. Kubal woke me to say that there was an emergency call for ambulances for a jeep accident, and that the victims would be arriving shortly, but that he could not find the medical officer of the day. I went out to 'Hammock Lane,' roused old liver lips (the commanding officer) from his comfortable retreat, and together we arrived at the receiving tent just as the ambulances were returning.

"They unloaded several soldiers and on a stretcher was the MP captain who had pasted Baldy. We could not believe that our prayers had been answered so soon. Gus quickly decided that he could use a few experts and we sent for the surgical team of Baker, Nethery and Mihalic. The MP captain, in viewing this collection of talent and vengeance lapsed into a coma.

"Baker, in his gentle examination, determined that the Captain had not been circumcised, and as regulations permitted any physician in the tropics to order a circumcision, ordered the procedure forthwith. Black Jack noted that no one knew the Captain's religious preference, and to be on the safe side, a proper authority should be consulted. Jim Coloin was pressed into service and with proper attire, book and machete gave, with a great deal of interruption and interpretation by the others, the ritual. At sun up I gave up, but at the next noon, while passing Baldy's tent, I observed him sleeping with a look of lovely pleasure on his bruised face." [2]

Later on, Gray tells what became of the trio.

"Later when we moved to Owi (island), Billy B. swam out to rescue some boys from a downed bomber, got a medal, went off his rocker, was sent home and died. Black Jack took to bourbon or whatever else was handy — was sent home to die (he didn't die until years later). Baldy died in July of this year" (1989).

The first two men were obvious casualties of the frenetic pace and near impossible task of saving thousands of lives amid the worst imaginable conditions. These men, like most of the doctors in the 92nd, took their jobs very seriously, showing little tolerance for bureaucracy or anything else that interfered with the best possible care for their patients.

Gray goes on to describe the enlisted men.

"Most of them were young, in their late teens or early twenties and came from a wide range of states. Most came from small towns or rural areas with few skills, training or education. They were amazed to find that the Army provided them with free clothing, room & board, some wages and a place to complain."[2]

The conditions under which the 92nd was expected to operate during 1944-45 were almost unbelievable. Tropical heat, jungle moisture and disease, the ever-present threat of Japanese attack and a continual struggle for essential supplies conspired to take both a physical and mental toll upon them. Yet somehow, this group came together, and was able to sustain a very high level of patient care throughout the war.

It seemed there were always shortages of needed items. "Scrounging" for these necessary commodities became essential to the smooth operation of the hospital. At Hollandia for example, the supply staff hatched a clever plan that would enable the group to get fresh meat from the Navy ships nearby. They began making "Jap flags" by painting bright red "meatballs" on white bed sheets with Mercurochrome, two commodities for which the 92nd had ample supplies, and trading these "souvenirs" for fresh meat. This bartering, had become SOP in the 92nd as it was for so many American units during WWII. Expertise in this discipline was not only admired, it was expected. [3]

Fr. Kilian was keenly aware of the necessity of this type of activity. That's why he specifically requested that he be quartered with the supply officer (Gray). Fr. Kilian wasn't above "appropriating" badly needed supplies either. Once when he and Gray had "appropriated" a critical generator from the Air Force nearby, Gray showed up at Fr. Kilian's tent the next morning saying excitedly, "Father, you just can't trust anyone any more. Those Air Force bastards came last night and stole it back." [3]

The 92nd was also unusual in that they had young women in their ranks. These nurses took the same risks as the men, and as you will see in the chapters ahead, the risks were very real. All of the nurses were officers and were forbidden to "fraternize" with the enlisted men. However, they worked side-by-side with many of them. They also participated fully in social and entertainment activities like dances, USO shows and athletic events. The 92nd's best softball pitcher was a nurse, Althea "Little Willy" Williams.

The contributions of these brave women have never truly been recognized or appreciated by most Americans. They sacrificed nearly as much as the men of the 92nd, and spent their share of time ducking into foxholes. However, almost all of them viewed this period of their lives as a remarkable adventure, which they would not trade for anything. Nurse Betty "Griffy" McCully recalls,

"Boy do I remember dear, blessed Putman trying to teach us nurses how to march. She did a marvelous job considering that a lot of us had two left feet. Anyway, I know I did. I hope we did her proud when we marched in Brisbane, at least I was proud of us.

"I remember the ward men who took such good care of the very, very sick patients with Typhus, carrying water from the bay to soak the sheets put around the patients to bring their temps down.

"Most of all, I remember the patience and tolerance of those around me for all my ignorance, immaturity and inexperience. I remember that friendships were forged that are (some) of the best of my lifetime. And last but not least, I remember people who made an experience that could have been traumatic for me, into an experience that was a thoughtful and maturing event." [4]

The 92nd would be a very busy hospital over the next 18 months. At the heart of this dedicated group of individuals was "The Padre," Fr. Kilian Dreiling. During his time with the 92nd, Fr. Kilian would go far beyond the basic tasks for which chaplains were trained. He knew the officers and enlisted men better than anyone did and he had a special love for the enlisted men. He developed a sense for what was needed and when it was needed most to keep the unit's morale high. The Company Commander usually followed his advice and counsel. Lt. Gray recalls Fr. Kilian's first day with the 92nd.

"...We were assigned a new chaplain. He arrived at the Great Breakfast Feast of fresh food from our raid on the USS Mizar (a supply ship that had run aground). He was sitting on a palm log in a poncho eating a rare fruit called an apple, and gazing with wonder and apprehension at his new flock. I sat with him awhile and he said he would like to have me for a room mate, and this became a turning point in my life.

"He became the de facto leader of the 92nd, and a friend and counselor to us all... He is a man worth loving." [5]

Chapter 9

The Invasion of Biak Island (No More Easy Victories)

After the nearly unopposed landings at Hollandia, McArthur's Army would face one of its most severe tests during the invasion of Biak Island. Biak was a strategic target because of its three airfields. From here, American long-range B-24 Liberator bombers would be able to reach the Philippines. McArthur was very anxious to strike back at the Japanese, who were committing unspeakable horrors upon the American soldiers that he had been forced to leave behind in the Philippine Islands. [1]

The Japanese too knew the strategic importance of Biak, and they had plenty of time to fortify the island. Several thousand Japanese troops were dug in among the caves that overlooked the eastern approaches to the island. Heavy guns, mounted on tracks, could be fired, and then retracted into the mountain caves. The landing itself was one of the most fiercely opposed of the war for McArthur's 6th Army. However, MacArthur's meticulous planning and superior firepower were too much for the Japanese defenders.

The assault Began with a 19-minute barrage from Rear Admiral William M. Fechteler's cruisers and destroyers. This was followed up by waves of B-24 Liberator bombers, attacking fortified positions and laying smoke to cover the invasion force. Small landing craft and barges then zigzagged their way through the surf to land infantry on the beaches. After the Japanese mortars and machine guns opened up on the troops, American rocket boats moved in to rain more destruction upon the defenders. American tanks began landing under this covering fire and began moving inland. Within 4-1/2 hours after the invasion began American Sixth Army troops were 2-1/2 miles inland and driving toward the first airfield. [1]

At this point however the Americans started encountering

increasingly stiff Japanese resistance. The fighting was fierce and the American advance became stalled. Bad weather did not help, as it kept badly needed U.S. air power grounded for a time. A rare tank battle even occurred as the Japanese clung tenaciously to Mokmer Air Drome. American Sherman tanks knocked out 11 Japanese tanks and continued the offensive. American casualties were heavy.

The 92nd was immediately put to the test. The hospital was working around the clock, situated in-between the front lines and the American artillery some 250 yards behind them. They were frequently bombed and strafed by Japanese planes, and witnessed dozens of air battles overhead. They even witnessed a Japanese zero pilot bail out and parachute within their own lines. [2]

For Fr. Kilian Dreiling, this period was truly a "baptism of fire." His reflections upon this battle speak of his personal experiences of the true horrors of war. Fr. Kilian recorded the following notes in a letter dated Sept. 7, 1944.

"I will never forget that battle. It was horrible! For two solid weeks our operating tables were going day and night. Raids and bombing became so common that we would not even stop our work."

A letter he sent back to the C.PP.S. order in Carthagena was written with the memories of the Biak battle still fresh in Fr. Kilian's mind. Later, it was published in the C.PP.S. newsletter, which was designed to keep all of the chaplains appraised of the experiences of their fellow priests around the world.

"Four days ago I came back from the front. The siege was long and most nerve-wracking. After a few days rest my nerves relaxed and with it came a weariness the like of which I have never experienced before. At first I dreaded to reflect what the results might be, but today I feel like my old self. It is about time to depart again, this time perhaps for an even greater grind.

"Nearly a hundred letters were awaiting me upon my return. Among them were orders to transfer to the 41st Division. My address however, remains the same. I regret the change, because of all that the old crowd had gone through together. It will mean going up with men I do not know. But in danger that does not make much difference. The immediate future does not look very bright. We go in again on Z day. (another code name for an assault on the enemy.) The brunt of the task will rest upon our group. I know no fear, but I cannot make myself take all this lightly.

"Life becomes as cheap as the dust upon which we walk. Blood becomes as common upon the hungry, ugly earth as the rains that wash it away. The remains of the dead meet a fate that crush the sensibilities of any sane, Christian man. Father Wuest was minutely correct when he said that war is hell. It is ghastly. It is terrible. It suddenly turns men cruel, even paganly ruthless. Men's simple minds seem to become overpowered with a diabolical influence that destroys all sense of balance and reason. It is difficult to say to what extent it is their own fault...to date I have given the enemy dead the same rites as our own. I hope I will not live to see the day when I shall have hardened to the extent of refusing that. What a terrifying revelation man will experience on that day when he will see his fellow men not as Japs, or Germans, or American, or English, but as so many images of God...

"I have in my possession sacred vessels, badly damaged, which the men have gathered from the ruined mission church. The rescued missionaries and sisters, 120 in all, have been removed to safer territory. Today I sent...my assistant, by boat to bring them whatever linens I could spare. And now Father, I shall prepare for Mass. Confessions are endless and Communions without number. I sometimes have to break the hosts into three or four pieces. May God bless you and all the members of our community." [3]

Many years later, Fr. Kilian would describe this period as a major turning point in his life. This next article, written as a sermon, shows how Fr. Kilian had to face and overcome his worst childhood fear: being in the presence of the dead. During the height of the battle for Biak, Fr. Kilian would later say that he buried more men in a single day than were buried in the entire Desert Storm campaign. He would literally work beyond exhaustion, totally immersed in his mission of caring for the dying and preparing the dead for burial.

"Greater Love Hath No Man..."

The message of Blood from the time of Abel to the last shedding of our present conflicts is ever the same, and yet, diverse as the gift of tongues. At the mere sight of blood, some fainthearted soul swoons, others gather courage, and still others turn into vicious animals, while the more gentle souls simply agonize with profound compassion and even grateful love. Indeed, the language of Blood, like the human smile, is most interpretive. I have seen them all, especially in the battlefield and concentration camps. But one dimension I came to know the hard way, the cruelest way, but in the end, the happiest way, I dare to say, even the blessed way.

Already as a child, I feared nothing more than a dead person. This ugly tormentor haunted me into adulthood and eventually followed me into the fiercest battles.

It all came about thus: During one of the bloodiest, not among the bloodiest, but the bloodiest invasions, casualties rolled in from all directions and at all times, day or night. Real military organization had not yet been established. We played the sad game totally by ear; did things completely contrary to military regulations. It was at this point of utter confusion that my Commanding Officer came to me and pleaded with me, that I not only care for the dying, but the dead. Would I, with all the enlisted help I wanted, recover from the dead personal belongings, clean the dead of blood, lay them out as best I could? In short, prepare them with some semblance of dignity for burial. At first sight I cringed. I literally recoiled. I wanted no part of this gory business. On second thought however, I decided to do what I had done many times before under similar circumstances; I betook myself to my tent and there pondered the weight of the request and my boundened duty.

After nearly an hour of deliberation and agonizing, compassion, duty and love prevailed. I forged ahead, bearing down on my fear like a wild animal. Suddenly, my aversion turned into unexpected compassion, sympathy and even intense love for the dead. Within an hour the gory task became a holy task. By lunchtime I could walk coolly and calmly across the road, step into the ocean, sit on a rock and slowly but reverently wash the human blood off my arms into the ocean. Often the blood of my comrades reached all the way to my shoulders. As I carefully washed the sacrificial blood into the ocean, a tremendous flood of sadness and compassion encompassed my entire body, and gored my very soul. With it also came a fuller, a clearer perception and understanding of the meaning of blood, especially human blood. The blood now mingled with the eternal ocean, became the ultimate and total sacrifice my dead soldier would, and did, give me and his country. It signified his life, the whole of it, offered in conjunction with the terrible sorrow of his mother, relatives and friends, it identified totally and completely with our Lord's saying, "Greater love than this no man hath than to lay down his life for his friends." If beautifully summed up: compassion, love and sacrifice.

The shedding of blood became the more noble because it was shed without a murmur or resentment, on an island far, far distant from home and country, and everlastingly treacherous and strange. True, occasionally a dying soldier would weakly complain, "Father, why must I die so far from home and on this stinken', rotten' island?" But this MILD complaint only intensified the impact on my soul. Often I would give way to the only relief available — I wept for the dead, their mothers and relatives. But above all I often and deeply pondered, and for long hours, the miraculous change of attitude I now maintained from the one I so tenaciously harbored a few days ago and even from childhood. I recall for example the night I unintentionally fell asleep caring for a dying soldier. I was tired, weary, frustrated, and sorrowful from endless nights without sleep. I awoke the next morning to the whispering of my assistants debating whether to awaken me or leave me to much more needed sleep. When I finally awoke fully, I realized that I had rested my head on a dead soldier's body but accepted it as entirely usual and with gratitude, only to begin another day just like yesterday and just like the tomorrow and every other tomorrow thereafter.

Nothing so affected me as to see the blood of the dead mingle with the vast ocean and float away and still farther away. Always I hoped and prayed that eventually it would find its way to the closest ocean to his home. Often too, I would sit by the grave, dangle my legs into the grave and offer to God his total sacrifice and in return, ask a merciful Father to grant him and all who slept beside him eternal peace — namely a peace that the world would not and could not give him; or that Jesus would gather all the souls in his mantle and carry them to the bosom of his heavenly Father. The burden, namely that I had to accept this ordeal in the name of the mother, relatives, wives or children was almost unbearable.

In conclusion, may I say what the blood of my dead soldiers did for me, and that the effect is almost worse today, some fifty years later. It purified my soul. It gave me courage unknown until then. It fortified me to be kind, understanding, compassionate, enduring, but above all through this terrible travail was born something so noble, so real that today I relate to it all in the same intense feeling and agony — love of the dead.

But now let me present my commentary on the above in the form of a challenge. Yes, in the light of all the above, do we perhaps more clearly see the wisdom of our heavenly Father in sending his Divine Son to shed his blood for you and me, and indeed, for all his creatures, our brothers and sisters in Christ? Do we see perhaps more clearly why he sheds his blood in every Eucharistic offering from the rising of the sun to its setting? Do we hopefully understand more fully the words of Peter, "You were redeemed not by worthless silver and gold, but by the precious blood of Christ?" Do we really realize that to worship Jesus and his Blood we must give ourselves to a deeper study, a fuller knowledge of the doctrine and devotion of the Most Precious Blood? Can we identify now more clearly with the beautiful song in singing, "Louder still louder to the praise of the Precious Blood?" Do we understand why our founder, St. Gaspar was impelled to cry out to all his sons, "For this I am priest — to apply the merits of the Precious Blood?"

Oh God, grant us this extraordinary grace!!! We pray to the Lord...Lord hear our prayer.

Fr. Kilian would emerge from his experiences on Biak a very changed man. The "epiphany" he experienced would allow him to replace his "fear of the dead," with a deeper "love for the dying and the dead." He began to see the supreme sacrifices that these young men were making as the ultimate act of love, and saw parallels between their sacrifices and the sacrifices made by Jesus Christ almost 2,000 years earlier. His order, the Precious Blood Society, believes passionately that only through the shedding of Christ's blood are we redeemed. That is why he titled this article, "Greater Love Hath No Man..."

Increasingly, Fr. Kilian would also come to respect these young men, not only for their bravery and resolution in the face of imminent danger, but for their ability to suffer hardships so far from the comforts of home and family as well.

One harrowing incident occurred when the battle for Biak was still in doubt. One evening, the 92nd was informed that large elements of the Japanese Navy were heading for their island. The report was true. A large Japanese naval force consisting of cruisers and destroyers were escorting several troop transports in an effort to reinforce their own beleaguered troops on Biak. The American navy would not be able to reach Biak before the Japanese ships, resulting in an inevitable naval bombardment, followed by troop landings. This could have turned the tide of the war in New Guinea in favor of the Japanese. Jim Colvin of the 92nd recalls this incident vividly.

"We received some very alarming news. We were told that at any time we could be given orders to destroy and/or bury our files and retreat inward into the jungles, where incidentally, the Japanese were located. Imagine a hospital unit having to fight and survive jungle warfare. It was communicated to us that practically the entire Japanese naval armada was coming down through the straits and not too many of our ships and planes were available to stop them. We sweated, suffered and waited for what seemed like an interminable interval of time before the news had filtered back that our naval and air force had turned the enemy back. And so ended one of our most tense and gripping experiences of the war."[4]

Fortunately for the Americans on Biak, General McArthur was able to scramble together 70 planes from U.S. airfields further down the New Guinea coast. These B-25 Mitchell medium bombers, escorted by fighter planes caught the Japanese ships only 100 miles to the Northwest of the island. Four Japanese destroyers were sunk and another was severely damaged, causing the rest of the fleet to flee.

Finally, the American fleet appeared on the horizon to the great relief of the members of the 92nd. [1]

Before the American planes came to their rescue however, the 92nd began fleeing into the hills. Many of the severely wounded had to be left behind, along with several of the doctors. Fr. Kilian volunteered to stay with them despite the pleadings of his fellow officers. He asked the soldiers to leave him a bucket of hand grenades. When Fr. Kilian was asked, "What are you going to do with them?" He replied, "Never mind son, as long as there is a grenade left in the barrel they're not going to touch my boys." [5]

The bloody battle for Biak would, many years later, inspire Fr. Kilian to record several more events that he felt should be remembered. The next episode occurred early in the battle, when Fr. Kilian had been called to the front lines. The battle was especially fierce at this point. Even the jeep ride to the front was dangerous. Japanese guns and mortars looked down upon the coastal road from the hills above.

"The Thunderous, Ever Haunting Whisper"

Biak is one of seven small islands directly north of New Guinea proper. From the sky, the complex of islands looks much like a mother hen with her sprawling chicks. The chicks are historically known as the "Schouten Islands." Biak is the largest of the seven and measures some 741 square miles. It is a totally dense jungle and at night as black as Satan's soul. Along the northern coast a cliff runs some four to five hundred feet high, as perpendicular as a dessert candle. In fact, parts of it extend over the angry ocean and openly defy it. The cliffs are honeycombed with countless and vast caves, much like underground prairie dog apartments. It was in these caves that the Japanese stored their ammunition, mountain guns, food, and ran their kitchens and laundries, as well as housing their sleeping quarters.

The mountain guns ran on tracks much like our railroad trains. Routinely, the enemy would release a salvo from the mouth of one cave, only to quickly retake itself far down the line. By the time we located the exact mouth from which the salvo came and responded in kind, the Japanese would be a mile down the tracks, only to repeat still another discharge. Past these caves to the far northeast lay the airstrip, Mokmer Airdrome. To this day, it looks much like a huge cereal bowl cut in half, with a circular, rising cliff on the right and the wide open ocean on the left. It especially was strategically well and intensely fortified.

The distance between the airstrip and our Evacuation Hospital was perhaps two miles. When the tide was in the airstrip was accessible only by water; namely, the ocean. When the tide was out we could reach the airstrip by land; namely, the improvised bedrock road along a two mile cliff.

It was precisely during the endless siege of the airstrip that my friend, Archie Roosevelt, (Teddy's youngest son), and his 162nd battalion were pinned down.* It was during this prolonged campaign that an intermittent but urgent SOS came from a Navy ship sitting in the bay. Over and over it flashed, "A Catholic chaplain urgently wanted up front."

No longer able to endure the plea, my Commanding Officer came to me and said, "Padre, a Catholic chaplain is urgently wanted up front, but there must be many Catholic chaplains between here and the airstrip. Do you feel it your duty to go?" I said, "Colonel, sir, it is not a matter of feeling, it is a matter of duty. I will go."

Quickly, I summoned my assistant, Mel. He was not only a great driver, but could read the compass equally well. I could not. About 11:30 PM, we began our safari. Slowly and ever so cautiously, we

---

* Fr. Kilian's friend Archibald "Archie" Roosevelt was the fifth child of former U.S. President Theodore Roosevelt. He served with distinction as a Captain during WWI and as a Lt. Colonel in WWII. Seriously injured in both wars, he earned numerous honors and holds the distinction of being the only American soldier who qualified for 100% disability from both world wars. Initially, Archie was unable to obtain a commission from the U.S. Army during WWII due to his disability. However, after enlisting the assistance of his first cousin, President Franklin Roosevelt, he was re-commissioned and served in the pacific as Commander of the 162nd Infantry, 41st Division. The 92nd Evacuation Hospital was attached to the 41st Division, and this is likely how Archie Roosevelt and Kilian became acquainted. Archie was wounded during the New Guinea campaign, and almost certainly spent time recuperating with the 92nd. [6]

hugged the cliff as we groped for two miles toward our goal. The headlight was only a sliver, about the size of a lead pencil and only an inch long. The road naturally was understandably dangerous. First, we well knew that at every gaping mouth of every cave sat the enemy on the lookout. Also, the waves perpetually washed rocks and debris into our improvised bedroad; or another vehicle, coming from behind in too great a hurry might accidentally ram into us. Still another coming toward us might ram us head-on. Caution was not only a command, it was wisdom on the march and survival the reward.

We finally arrived at the airport without incident or mishap, but were still a far way from our goal. We inquired at every orderly room in the hope that we might find help. At last, indeed at long last, we crawled into the right orderly room. A young, dedicated medic knew the location, but even better, was most anxious to lead us to the exact spot. It was a dreadfully hot and humid, dark night, and the excitement of groping through so much dangerous jungle added and intensified the discomfort. But, it was our reward. We found the lad who persisted on seeing a Catholic chaplain.

Without any preliminary preparation, I quickly heard the soldier's confession, and added for good measure, all the extra Rites of the Church. And he? Now at peace with his Creator and his own soul, surrendered. Most unceremoniously, he crossed the divide. This behavior I so often found in dying solders, no matter what their religion or nationality.

However, long before I concluded the rites of the dying soldier, the faithful medic frantically urged me to hurry as he pleaded, "There are many more." Obediently, I complied and at once set out for my next casualty. I had only taken a few steps when a painfully distorted voice penetrated the very marrow of my bones. It was a hurt voice, an urgent voice, indeed, a pleading voice. Though it came in a suppressed whisper, it resounded like a fiery bolt out of the clear and with the force of a thousand tornadoes.

"And Father, you are NOT going to pray with me?" I instantly got down on my knees and desperately said, "Soldier, just exactly where are you?" He replied, "Father, I am right next to you." And for a second time in minutes, I bent over a dying soldier. Both were terminally wounded and could be moved only with the greatest of care.

As I held his hand firmly in my hands, I said, "Soldier, what is your religion?" With a touch of anger he hesitatingly replied, "Father, I have no religion." Slowly and cautiously, I asked, "And what kind of prayer do you want me to say with you?" I so hoped he would at least say "The Lord's Prayer." Instead, I heard a harsh voice, a judgmental voice, an accusing voice, indeed a bitter voice. "Father, my parents never taught me one single prayer in all my life." Then, realizing my total embarrassment, he took my hand in both of his and pleaded, "Father, would you consider saying the same prayers over me that you just said over my now dead pal?"

Quickly, I reached for my canteen, baptized him immediately, and added all the prayers for the dying. Later, I was told that he too, surrendered his soul on the way to the portable hospital.

But note: This was only the beginning of the campaign to secure the island. The days and weeks that followed proved even more cruelly venturesome. Truth is, it was on this island that I buried as many as 23 in five minutes, and I buried every hour on the hour during the daylight.

Now, fifty years later, the impact of this haunting whisper remains as fresh in my memory as the eternal breath of God Himself. Over and over I agonize over this incident because it still opens the doorway to countless occasions, and other episodes even sadder than these. Often, and seriously I ask myself, "How could I live with myself if my dying son or daughter had accused me of failing to teach them about their God and Creator, or even to pray?" It is indeed a thought to ponder.

But a soldier in the battlefield does not only die for his parents, or wife or children. He makes the heroic sacrifice for his country, for his countrymen. In brief, for you America!!!

And, what do we parents, wives, friends, countrymen, yes, we America do for him in return? We thoughtlessly, yes even cruelly deprive him or her of the only thing that counts when we come to die; namely, the gift to know, love and serve God our Creator. To belong to a blind and liberal society, we fail to teach him or her even one, single prayer. Indeed, the simplest and merest knowledge necessary to save his or her soul.

What did the prophet, a famous TV preacher, predict before WWII? "The tragedy is not that thousands of fine young men and women will die in the battlefield. The tragedy is that many, many will die like sheep at the slaughter, not knowing even the value of his or her own soul, much less the value of his or her God and Creator.

Parents, wake up!!! Countrymen, wake up!!! Yes, America wake up!!! The hour is late indeed. The hour is at hand, if not passed.

After Fr. Kilian's actions at the battle of Biak the members of the 92nd began to see him as "fearless." One dying soldier at the front urgently desires to see a Catholic chaplain and, after dodging sniper fire, Fr. Kilian appears. He derived great satisfaction from helping young soldiers find peace before their God so that they could enter his heavenly kingdom without fear. Fr. Kilian truly found his calling in the jungles of New Guinea by quietly and calmly reassuring the young men in their final hours. There would be many more incidents where Fr. Kilian would put his own life on the line to come to the aid of a dying soldier. He is credited with savings several lives. One of these incidents occurred on Biak.

During the middle of an otherwise "normal" day on Biak, the surgeons were at work when the calm was shattered by the "boom-boom-boom" of an anti-aircraft gun. Doctors and enlisted men, (the nurses had not been brought up yet), fully aware by now that this was the air raid alert signal, began diving for cover. My father, Joe "Smitty" Smith, recalled crawling underneath a truck and seeing a diving Japanese airplane making a strafing run. Bullets were churning up the sand all around him, when he saw a gunner from a nearby anti-aircraft battery exchanging fire. Suddenly, the 50 caliber guns from the quad mount fell silent as the American gunner slumped over in his harness. The plane then dropped a bomb in the middle of the 92nd's compound.

After the terrifying explosion, Fr. Kilian was the first to emerge from cover. He frantically ran around making sure everyone was all right. He noticed the tip of an M-1 carbine rifle sticking out of the sand and began digging with his hands. With the help of several others, Fr. Kilian unearthed a grateful little Kentuckian nick-named "Jeep" and another companion. Both had nearly suffocated and were rescued just in time after diving into a slit trench that was soon to become a latrine. [7]

Later, Fr. Kilian would remember this incident, but not the names of the men he had rescued. Some 40 years later, in the unlikeliest of places, Fr. Kilian would again come face to face with one of these men. "Jeep" would forever remember the man who had saved his life.

Fr. Kilian's constant concern for the soldiers and nurses caused others to compare him to a "mother hen" looking after her chicks. On one occasion, the soldiers in the hospital had no cigarettes to smoke. This was a critical shortage in 1944 when so many of the men considered cigarettes a necessity.

Fr. Kilian, moved by the men's discomfort, was compelled to act. He summoned Chaplain's Assistant Smith, and asked him to drive him down to the beach where the Navy LST's (designation for "landing ship, tanks"), were docked. After receiving permission from each ship's captain, Fr. Kilian took the loudspeaker and addressed the crew saying,

"Look here boys, we've got a lot of wounded and dying men in our hospital that don't even have a cigarette to smoke. Now I know each of you has a duffel bag full of cigarettes down below. When he noticed men laughing he said, "I'm not kidding! I'm only asking for half of what you've got" [7]

They filled the jeep with cigarettes. When the Red Cross representative asked Fr. Kilian if he could have a few boxes, Fr. Kilian rebuked him saying, "You get your own damn cigarettes! Our boys won't be buying these."

Fr. Kilian was not a fan of the Red Cross's tactics of selling necessities to the soldiers, and could quickly become indignant when he observed what he perceived to be injustice.

Chapter 10

The Owi Island Campaign,
a Different Enemy

When the American offensive on Biak Island stalled, the Sixth Army had yet to capture Mokmer Air Drome. They badly needed a forward air base to support the campaign. Nearby Owi island was completely uninhabited and so it was chosen as the best place to build an airstrip. One mile wide and one and a half miles long, it was just barely large enough for this purpose.

When the engineers landed on Owi, they noticed some partially complete native huts built on stilts at the water's edge. They were curious as to why the huts had never been finished, but nevertheless began building the much-needed airstrip immediately. In two weeks they had built a 7500 foot long air strip and the Fifth Air Force was sending out large groups of B-24 Liberators to bomb the Philippines with P-38 and P-47 fighter escorts. However, they would soon learn why the natives had referred to Owi as "Ghost Island." [1]

Dr. Joe Davis of the 92nd recalls what happened next.

"The Seabees did a phenomenal job of clearing out the jungle and making an airstrip in record time. The airstrip went the entire length of the island, with our hospital located on the beach at the exit end of the runway. The quarters of the Air Force units and Seabees were along the side of the strip.

"What was not known when we decided to use Owi, was that the island was infested with a mite that carried the Scrub Typhus, or Tsutsugamushi Fever. Soon our hospital was full of sick Seabees and Air Force personnel, some of them critically ill. We admitted over 1,000 cases and unfortunately, all we could do was to evacuate them to units in the rear." [2]

Unfortunately, for the sick men on Owi, no one knew why they were getting sick. Scrub Typhus was not only a very rare disease, it was a deadly one. It would take the heroic efforts of Dr. Armstrong and his dedicated staff to finally diagnose this disease. Going 36 hours without sleep, Armstrong scoured every medical book and manual available before identifying the disease. What he found horrified him. The survival rate for Scrub Typhus was estimated to be only 30%!

Dr. Armstrong issued strict orders to the nurses and ward men. The suffering men were to receive "absolute and total bed rest." Armstrong elaborated, "I don't want these men to lift a finger to get a drink of water!"[1] Sponge baths were prescribed to keep the fevers down. This was an exhausting task for a hospital whose 400 bed capacity had necessarily been doubled. Back and forth to the beach went the men to soak the sheets, in order to cool down the patients.

Members of the 92nd remember the Scrub Typhus epidemic vividly. The entire resources of the hospital were mobilized and focused on achieving one goal: providing these very sick men with the best possible care in order to increase their chances of survival. The rewards for this constant diligence were nothing short of remarkable. Out of over 1,200 men who succumbed to Scrub Tyhpus on Owi, only 12 cases were fatal.

The story of one of these unfortunate young men is told vividly by Fr. Kilian. He and another young nurse, who had cared for the young man, became very close to him. Fr. Kilian also recounts another close call he experienced, which added to his reputation as a fearless man of faith.

"Johnny Doe"

Our hospital tents or wards might correctly have been divided or classified between battle casualties or jungle casualties wards. My memory tells me that most of the jungle casualties were assigned to Lori's tents. I recall one night, when she had nine dying patients in one ward. Most cases (serious) were scrub typhus, jungle rot, amoebic dysentery, malaria or dengue fever. Lori watched over them all with the eagle eye of a guardian angel. Often when she feared that the patient would not make it through the night, she would approach him and say, "Son, you are very sick. Would you like for Father to come and pray with you?" Most often the wounded or sick soldier would reply, "But nurse, I am not Catholic." Lori would reply, "Oh son! I am not either, but if I were as sick as you are, I would crawl to his knees and plead with him to pray with me."

Consider that we had about 49 patients in each tent and in all, well over 40 tents. You may then evaluate my nightly routine. Many would refuse, or even defy the effects of the sleeping pills, until I had said my prayer with them. Eventually, it was taken for granted that praying with a dying or very sick soldier was a bounden duty on my part. Indeed it was.

Perhaps the most outstanding, the most celebrated, and most beautiful case was the case of John Bow (we nicknamed him Johnnie Doe). He was a stalwart 6'3" ariman, blond, muscular, kind, gentle and ever grateful. He came out of the very heart of New York City. Scrub typhus, the then unknown entity and enemy however, laid him low. It decimated his every cell, muscle and marrow. At the peak of his vacillating fever, he asked that I pray with him- nightly. I did, while Lori, R.N., stood over him and watched him like a huge mother-eagle-guardian angel. Truly, she was not only the spiritual support of Johnnie Doe's, but of me, her chaplain. At long last however, the fever broke and Johnnie showed signs of improvement. We all rejoiced gratefully. Still, no amount of dope would put him to sleep until I had said my prayers with him... or he with me. Johnnie Doe was fast on the road to recovery, for all to see.

But then came the unfortunate fatal day. It was a Sunday. I had started saying Mass at 6:00 AM on the extreme right end of the island. By noon, I would reach my hospital, eat lunch, and proceed to the other end of the island. Father Donnelly and I joined forces. When he had Mass and preached, I would hear confessions and help with communions. The last Mass was scheduled for 9:00 PM on the extreme opposite end of the island. It was a beautiful night and the attendance was heartwarming. After Mass with the area still brightly lit, we made for a much-deserved supper. However, before we reached the mess hall the yellow alert went off, and in the wake of the yellow came the red alert, and on the wings of the red came the bombers. We had not even found a foxhole when it all happened.

Bombs rained from heaven like hail. We hurried back to the area, and where only a few minutes before there reigned peace and tranquility and light, there now reigned havoc. We gazed in utter and absolute disbelief. The area was a veritable hellish slaughterhouse. The wounded were everywhere, and calls for help came from all directions. All naturally were Fr. Donnelly's people. At first sight, he simply froze, handed me the oils and pleaded with me to carry on. I mustered all the adrenaline, spiritual and physical, and plunged. Eventually, I came upon a huge foxhole. It was a veritable grave size foxhole. In it were twelve men. An anti-personnel bomb exploded about four feet above the foxhole and flattened it into a huge soup bowl. The bodies were literally slittered. By the time I reached the foxhole, some two to three hundred men had gathered around it. Impulsively I yelled, "Is there anyone alive in this foxhole?" The only response was the echo from the jungle. Ever so softly and insultingly, it mimicked me, "Is there anyone alive in this foxhole?" A second time I called and a second time the echo returned even more insultingly. "Is there anyone living in this foxhole?" Now, well fortified with adrenaline and a measure of anger, I plunged into the foxhole, quickly prayed over all, and then proceeded to give attention to individuals. In the center, I came upon a chaplain. (The affinity between chaplains was next to miraculous). Reverently, I lifted his head to see if there was life. The answer was instant. My fingers went through his brains to the opposite side of his skull. Still more kindly and reverently, I laid his head back in position as I wiped my fingers on my fatigues. A soldier standing at the edge of the foxhole went berserk and said, "These G.D. priests aren't afraid of anything." I looked up at him and said, "Son, I hope you will never forget that." He replied, "I will never, never forget this scene, nor will all who saw it." The response from the crowd came as one voice, "Never! Never! Padre and we thank you!"

My next concern — Fr. Donnelly. We brought him to his tent, put him to bed, but he was still stiff as a corpse in deep, cold storage. But a second time, still another silent, urgent call came from the opposite end of the island- my hospital.

The road leading to my hospital ran through much jungle. With reckless abandon, I deliberately defied all caution at intersections as I hastily returned with sinful haste. I parked my Jeep and made for the orderly room. Just then, the O.D., (Officer of the Day), emerged. Seeing me he threw up his arms, whimpered like a child asking its mother to lift him up and said, "Padre, you are dead, I mean you were reported dead in that foxhole." I calmly said, "Captain, come feel me, touch me, I am alive. He gave no answer. He simply put his head on my shoulder and wept. But time was of the essence.

Lori, RN, lost no time. She physically manhandled me and ordered me to come quickly to her ward. Johnnie had learned through the grapevine that I had been killed. He was slipping fast. Lori quickly clued me in on the way to her ward. One look at Johnnie and I saw that he was dying. With heroic effort he rested his hand on my shoulder, pulled my head close to his and asked to be baptized. Lori hurriedly gave me a canteen and I baptized Johnnie and added all the prayers of the dying.

Next morning, I said Mass with his body present, and when I suggested that we bury him the usual way, his unit nearly lynched me. No way was Johnnie to be buried in a sheet, poncho or blanket. He was to be buried in a wooden coffin, (of their own making). Ever so reverently, we laid him in his final earthly home. However, the body lay in state until all his unit had paid its respect. Before we carried him to the nearby cemetery, I lifted the removable board and standing over him tearfully said, "Johnnie, somehow, somewhere, sometime, I will find your mother, twin sister and family, and tell them all — namely, all about your departure to a better life and a better place."

Incidentally, Johnnie was only one of two dead soldiers I ever buried in a wooden coffin, and I buried sometimes more in one day than died in the whole of Desert Storm.

Fr. Kilian would keep his promise to Johnnie Doe as he did for so many brave young soldiers who had died in his arms.

Members of the 92nd frequently witnessed heroic incidents. One incident involving two doctors from the 92nd however, involved an act of heroism that no one would ever forget.

One of the B-24 heavy bombers that took off daily to bomb the Japanese in the Philippine Islands never gained enough altitude and crashed into the sea. The water was rough and there was a strong current separating Owi from Biak Island. Doctors Baker and Davis, without hesitation, dove into the ocean and braved the dangerous waters. Baker was able to rescue one of the floundering pilots and pull him safely to shore. He went back again, but could find no more survivors. He was devastated by his inability to do more. Baker would later receive a medal for bravery for this act. [3]

With close air support from the Fifth Air Force on Owi Island, the Sixth Army was able to push forward on Biak, capture all three airfields and secure the island. General Douglas MacArthur was now able to announce, "For strategic purposes, this marks the practical end of the New Guinea campaign... these operations have secured bases of departure for the advance to its vital areas in the Philippines and Netherlands East Indies." [4]

Once Biak was secured, things quieted down a great deal for the 92nd on Owi. A beautiful officer's club was built and there was time now for recreational activities like baseball, volleyball and horse-shoes. They were even treated to a USO show featuring Bob Hope, Frances Langford, Jerry Colona and others. A special toilet constructed for the female entertainers later bore the sign, "Frances Langford sat here." [5] Dr. Joe Davis would later recall some of the other activities the 92nd engaged in to fight boredom.

"Extracurricular activities here included making canoes out of discarded belly tanks and making snorkel masks out of Plexiglas and inner-tubes. There were a lot of tropical fish in the lagoon, which we would try to spear. The natives soon learned to fish by throwing a grenade into the water. The force of the explosion would kill a bunch of fish and bring them to the surface at the same time.

"There were many dog-fights at night between our Black Widows (P-61 night fighters) and the Jap planes. It was exciting to see the trail of tracer bullets from our fox holes." [5]

On another occasion, members of the 92nd watched as a small, unarmed army observation plane was bounced and surprised by a Japanese Zero fighter. After luring the Japanese pilot down to treetop level, the army pilot flew dangerously close to a hillside, pulling up at the absolute last second. The Japanese pilot, flying at high speed, could not pull up and exploded into the hillside in a ball of flame. The U.S. pilot would later paint a small Japanese flag on the side of his airplane, thereby claiming his first, and probably only "kill" of the war. [1]

One activity organized by Fr. Kilian was quite memorable for all of the enlisted men. Fr. Kilian had a way of seizing or creating opportunities at just the right time to boost morale. He was also adept at getting his way with the Company Commander. During a slow period, Fr. Kilian suggested and received permission to hold a "Nurses and enlisted men's dance." This was completely against the "no fraternization" regulations, but it provided a rare respite for the common soldier, and an opportunity to remind them that they were still young men, capable of having the kind of fun they had become accustomed to before the war. Through these types of thoughtful acts, Fr. Kilian endeared himself to all in the 92nd, regardless of rank or gender. [1]

Fr. Kilian's love for adventure and powers of persuasion would allow him to pursue more exciting forms of entertainment. 42 years later he would record one such event in one of his many X-Mas letters.

"...whenever an island was quite secure and time lagged, we became bored. To relieve the boredom, I would plead with the Air Force pilots, whom I also served, to take us on a daring air-flight safari. Most often they obliged, but not without hesitation and fear. Once, we were even treated to a most unusual experience: a glider ride dry-run. Also with horror, I recall 40 years later, that I personally, a chaplain, flew a B-24 over much of New Guinea with reckless abandon. My doctors, all accomplices, encouraged me to fly lower and lower, the better to see the jungle, monkeys, crocodiles and raging rivers and by chance, a hiding savage. By some divine protection, we managed always to return home safely."

As always, Fr. Kilian's sense of humor was ever present. On one occasion, he enlisted the assistance of nearly every Catholic in the 92nd to participate in a practical joke he played on another Catholic Chaplain, Fr. McManus who served with a nearby Seabee company.

Inter-service rivalries often spawned such activities. When Fr. McManus came to assist Fr. Kilian with the usual Wednesday night Novena confessions, Fr. Kilian made sure that all of the Catholics in his company lined up to confess their sins to Fr. McManus. After an unusually long night of hearing many confessions, Fr. McManus finally caught on to the scheme. Eventually, he refused to grant absolution to one nurse, Leona Cote when she could not come up with any "real sins" telling her, "Go out and commit some sins and then come back." As Nurse Cote began to leave the church, she genuflected and began laughing so hard that she could not get back up. Fr. Kilian then approached Nurse Cote and discovered what had just happened. His response to her was, "Well, maybe you can go kill a few Japs and then come back and see Fr. McManus."

As casualties from the Biak Island campaign declined, more began to arrive from battles raging in Saipan, from jungle diseases and from accidents. Once, two native boys on Owi tripped a hand grenade mine and suffered calf wounds. A native chief cleaning out an oil drum with gasoline caught on fire and later died from his wounds. Subsequently, members of the 92nd witnessed an unusual spectacle. A funeral procession of war canoes was held for the chief, which was attended by the entire tribe. [5]

Father Kilian's next story is from this period. It reminds us that the dangers of operating a forward air base are not limited to the pilots and aircrew. This tender tale speaks of one young soldier's love for his dear friend, and his reliance on his own faith.

"He Bleeds — My Friend Bleeds"

The time was late in the afternoon on Biak Island, due north of New Guinea. The sun was readying to plunge into the western horizon in all its glory and fury. I was, aimlessly but apprehensively, drifting from ward to ward, awaiting any moment the onslaught when the wounded would be brought into our hospital undercover of darkness. They would arrive in jeeps, weapons-carriers, trucks of all sorts. My position at that specific time was critical — the receiving tent. However, my meandering and concern was instantly interrupted. A runner suddenly rushed upon me and for all to hear, cried in alarm, "Father, you are desperately wanted in surgery." Together, we straddled tent pegs, tent ropes, not to mention clothes hanging on the ropes to dry.

As I entered surgery, the doctors automatically stepped aside and anxiously said, almost in unison, "Father, he is Catholic." After a momentary hesitation, as I looked for a proper place to anoint, I simply plunged and anointed what may well have been his lower chin, and asked questions later. To this day I wish that I had never asked the questions.

The soldier in question, anxious to serve and save his country, faked his age. Even now only a few months before the final surrender, he was only seventeen. He was attached to the B-24 group as a maintenance man. Excited about getting a B-24 on the runway in its proper place and time, he accidentally backed into the powerful propeller of the B-24. The blade sheared nearly half of his head as clean and precise as mother used to slice bread. His death of course was imminent, only a matter of minutes, so we all thought. But the young, vigorous, dedicated body created a paradox. He refused to die. Instead, he bled and bled, and after that, bled still more — and lived. The doctors did not assign him to a ward. They simply placed him outside the surgery tent on a litter. In the event of any sign of pain, they would quickly administer morphine.

I, in the meantime, returned to the receiving tent, but periodically returned to my bleeding solder boy to pray that God would quickly take his soul. Through all of this, the soldier boy just kept bleeding and bleeding. His head by now looked like a huge basketball. With every additional wrapping of gauze the bleeding momentarily stopped, only to reappear with still greater force. It trickled onto the stretcher and from there it followed a tiny rivulet that flowed into the soft, white coral and left a glaring circle.

The sun by now had dropped behind the horizon. Strict blackout was severely enforced. During the respites in the receiving tent, I continued to look in on my bleeding soldier boy. About 10:00 PM I made still another dash to note his condition. To my consternation he was nowhere to be found. He vanished, it seemed, into mid-air. The help in the surgery tent were as puzzled as I was. Deeply disturbed now, I went in search by myself. In back of surgery was a huge foxhole, larger than a grave, but only three feet deep. Also in the tent was a tiny hole. Through it a beam of light pointed directly into the foxhole. There, sitting against the wall of the foxhole, was his friend, holding him in his arms and weeping bitterly. With one hand, he dangled a rosary in his friend's faceless form, and between compassionate sobs, he tolled his beads. The scene was so totally sacred that under no circumstances would I disturb it. From afar I joined in his prayer. Time and again he shifted the head of his friend, hoping to stop the bleeding, only to have it reappear more vigorously.

I invited all in surgery to quietly witness the sad but sacred scene. All returned stone sober and in tears

About midnight, I returned for the last time. Our noble soldier boy was dead. However, before leaving, his friend laid him out in the bottom of the foxhole, crossed his fingers in prayer, and tied them with still another rosary. Totally unbelievable, blood still oozed through the gauze, slowly congealed on the stretcher or at last on the white coral.

The next morning we brought his remains, as well as all who died during the night, to our chapel where I offered Mass for all. Our soldier boy was finally at rest. Even his blood was at peace. It flowed no longer.

The impact of this experience has been a lifetime in dying. It imbued and aroused in me a greater desire to know and love the P.P.S. (Most Precious Blood) of Jesus. Like our Lord, he shed his blood for God and all countrymen. Even as our Lord gave his last drop of blood in obedience to the thrust of a lance <u>in death</u>, so our soldier boy obediently gave his last drop of blood in <u>death</u>, not to the thrust of a spear, but the brutal blade of a B-24 propeller.

For both it was a total sacrifice- a complete sacrifice of love — a lasting proof that, "Greater love than this no man hath than to shed his blood for his friends."

The last few months on Owi Island were relatively quiet for the 92nd. By the time they left the island they had the "best equipment and the best operators on the island" according to supply officer

Lt. Gray. [6] This included New 5 KVA generators, which enabled the hospital to operate lighting, medical equipment, fans and even ice machines without major interruption. The generators were obtained when Gray "blackmailed" a nearby Corps of Engineer Major who he claims had been "buggering" one of his men.

When the B-24's weren't taking off or landing, the tropical nights, shimmering moonlight and the sound of the surf made Owi seem like anything but a war zone. Most members of the 92nd have fond memories of this period. Budding romances between nurses and other officers grew into the real thing, and on at least two occasions, ended in marriage. [1]

During all this time, MacArthur had been putting the finishing touches on his invasion plans for the Philippine Islands. His grand plan for liberating the Philippines was nearly shelved however, when MacArthur's naval counterpart, Admiral Chester Nimitz proposed an alternate plan, which would bypass the Philippine Islands entirely. Nimitz argued for a more direct path to Japan, which would leave the Japanese garrisons on the Philippines to wither on the vine, cut off from their bases of supply.

Douglas MacArthur however, was keenly aware that there were still thousands of American GI's in the Philippines being held prisoner. He felt a strong obligation to see not only his soldiers, but the Filipino people liberated as well. After all, he had promised them, "I shall return." As pre-war governor of the Philippines, MacArthur had developed a special bond with its people, and he did not want to see them suffer under Japanese oppression any longer. In the end, MacArthur prevailed after much pleading with President Roosevelt. The Philippine invasion was on.

On November 1st, the 92nd began staging operations for their departure. On December 24th, they boarded the Liberty Ship, "Charles Goodnight." [7] Christmas of 1944 was spent in the Aitape Harbor, awaiting assembly of the convoy, which would take them to the island of Luzon, P.I. It was probably the gloomiest Christmas any of them had ever experienced. Ahead lay a long sea voyage, an unpleasant experience that by now had become all too familiar. They also knew that at the end of this voyage and with each subsequent invasion, they were getting closer and closer to the Japanese homeland, and farther and farther away from home.

Fr. Kilian held Christmas Mass aboard ship. By now they were all veterans, and had become a close-knit group. Together, they had accomplished a great deal. They had saved thousands of lives, giving American soldiers the best possible care that the circumstances would allow. They performed an extremely vital function for MacArthur's 6th Army and they had every reason to be proud. The members of the 92nd had no idea what was in store for them as they set out once again upon the vast Pacific, their exact destination unknown. They were pretty sure however, that they were going to help General MacArthur fulfill his promise to the Philippine people.

The "Charles Goodnight" would sail with a large convoy consisting of some 46 Liberty Ships, 46 LST's and assorted naval escort vessels. What happened next would forever be recorded as a new and terrifyingly different phase of the Pacific War, and the 92nd and Fr. Kilian Dreiling would be right in the middle of it all.

Chapter 11

The Invasion of the Philippine Islands

For most of the three-week voyage from Owi Island to the island of Luzon, P.I. (Philippine Islands), the trip was comparatively uneventful. For most veteran soldiers and sailors, that's just how they like it. However, as they entered Leyte Gulf, they would encounter a terrifying new weapon employed by the Japanese out of desperation: the Kamikaze, or "Divine Wind" suicide attack planes. Fr. Kilian tells this story in his own words.

"For days we have been floating on the high seas, and now I am in the thick of it all." He adds, "The trip was calm and comparatively peaceful, but not entirely uneventful. I thought we had experienced almost everything. We had seen plane after plane explode, catch fire and plunge into the ocean or mountainside. We had seen planes catch fire in mid-air and race like lightning for some target. But the ace was reserved for this trip. For the first time we witnessed squads of suicide planes. There was no mistaking their deliberate purpose. They carried neither bombs nor strafing guns, only a human bomb. Like a bolt they would appear from behind a cloud and with cold determination dive for a ship. It was a ghastly sight. Their aim was pitiful. They would plunge into the sea and leave a wake of gushing gasoline, flame, smoke and debris on the water. After a moment of breathless excitement among those on board, there was a spontaneous outburst of joy, and another soul's destiny was decided." [1]

Jim Colvin of the 92nd also provides this dramatic account of the Kamikaze attacks, indicating just how close the "Charles Goodnight" and the 92nd came to becoming a casualty of this new and terrifying form of warfare.

"This particular day I was standing on the deck with Dr. Mancuso, idly watching the sea, when I noticed a plane speeding towards our position. I remember thinking and wondering why one of our planes would be doing such a stupid thing unless he was having trouble with his plane. Suddenly, it occurred to me that this plane was going to crash right into the side of the ship next to us. I stood hypnotized, unable to say a word or move. The explosion was tremendous and unbelievable! It seemed only moments later that the ship's prow just turned gently down into the water and disappeared. Then all hell broke loose as many more Japanese planes appeared in the sky, all converging on the 'coffin corner' (the unfortunate location of the Charles Goodnight). The noise from the 'ack-ack' fire was deafening and fearful. I suddenly experienced something I had seen in the movies — an individual completely mesmerized by the gyrations of a cobra before it struck. I was frightened but absolutely immobile. My senses told me, 'Go below,' but my mind was too fascinated by the spectacular, sensational display to give the order of retreat to my body. The attack did not last too long, but I remember seeing one plane that I was certain was destined to crash right into us. It did hit the ship right next to us with disastrous results." [2]

My father describes this same, terrifying event. Unable to stomach being crowded together in the bowels of the ship with hundreds of other poor, smelly souls, Kentuckian Sgt. Joe Smith was topside scanning the skies. Seeing a group of suicide planes flying at extreme altitude, he turned to a nearby anti-aircraft gunner and asked, "Could them be birds up there?" The response was swift, "Hell no, those are zeros!"

Calling into his voice tube, the gunner alerted gunnery command. "Bandits, eleven O'clock!" Suddenly, the skies lit up as every ship in the convoy began firing at the intruders. At this point, Smith decided he had better seek cover, fearing that the deck might soon be sprayed with bullets. The well through which the anchor chain passed looked like a good hiding place. However, after climbing down the anchor chain he vividly remembered the thought that suddenly crossed his mind.

"What if they have to stop this ship and drop anchor? I'd be riding this anchor chain down to Davey Jones's Locker!" [3]

With the words "Davey Jones's Locker" echoing in his head, Smith found a better hiding place; the blade of a bulldozer parked on deck. From here, he watched as the first Kamikaze crashed into the ship behind the Charles Goodnight. Suddenly, another plane, travelling at wave-top height to avoid the anti-aircraft fire, headed straight for the Goodnight. Following its zigzag course, the Goodnight suddenly "zagged," forcing the desperate Japanese pilot to miss his target. However, he was able to alter his course and plow straight into the ship directly in front of the Goodnight. This had to be the same plane that Jim Colvin was "certain" would crash into the Goodnight. [3]

After this narrow escape, the 92nd had landed on Luzon. Fr. Kilian would later comment: "From all appearances, the invasion is a pushover. Hard to believe! The Japs are queer...To date we have no air raids. Explain that if you can." [1]

"The explanation came later through 'Intelligence.' The following day that this letter was written, only ten of the Japanese aircraft remained on the entire island of Luzon. The rest were sent to Formosa (Taiwan). The ground crews were mustered into the Japanese infantry to help defend Luzon. They lost it." [1]

The American landings in the Lingayen Gulf came as a terrible surprise to the Japanese Army. This was the third landing in a little more than three weeks for the U.S. 6th Army. The first invasion site was at Leyte Gulf on the island of Leyte. The second invasion was at Mindoro on the large island of Luzon. The third landings at Lingayen were on the opposite (West) side of Luzon, placing a powerful American force behind the Japanese Army.

The 92nd landed in Lingayen Gulf at San Fabian and immediately established the hospital and began accepting patients. The beachhead was a relatively small area, with several units crowded together. Not very far away, Japanese soldiers were holed up in caves to the Northeast. Artillery was then brought up to get at them. Once again, the 92nd would be situated in-between the American artillery and the Japanese Army. Once again, they were dangerously close to the front lines. Three days after landing, 15 Japanese infantrymen intent on silencing the artillery, infiltrated the hospital area of the 92nd. Without warning, the Japanese attacked. Most of the hospital staff were sleeping and were rudely awakened by the sounds of rifle and machine gun fire. They suddenly found themselves in a close-quarters fight for their life!

It had been well over two years since basic training for most of these men, and few had ever fired a shot in anger. Confusion and chaos reigned for most of that evening. No one knew how many enemy soldiers had entered their compound, and most of the 92nd men took immediate shelter in foxholes and slit trenches without bothering to grab their rifles or ammunition. By now used to air raids, their natural instinct was to seek shelter. Joe Davis of the 92nd provides this chilling account of the events of January 19th, 1945.

"At about 1:00 A.M. I heard firing of small arms overhead. I jumped into a foxhole with a carbine. Jap voices were very close, lots of jabbering, MG and rifle fire. Japs had infiltrated our area, killed three (actually four) and injured six. The Japs threw grenades and one set off our supply dump. At about 2:00 A.M. the firing and sounds of Japs were gone and we got up to fight the fire. Lost most of our bedding and tents but not much else. Spent the rest of the night on the supply pile- what a long night. At dawn we went over and saw four dead Japs near the creek, less than 100 yards from where I was in the foxhole... We suffered one casualty when one of our best enlisted men, Sergeant (one of the four) was bayoneted in the groin while he was asleep in his cot. The wound apparently severed the common iliac artery and he bled to death almost immediately.

"As the supply pile was set afire, thus illuminating the sky, (Dr.) Cy Burroughs raised his head out of his foxhole to ask, 'What's going on here?' He was answered by a grenade, which fortunately, produced only a minor wound. Burroughs became the only officer of the 92nd to get a Purple Heart!"[4]

Killed during this action were Eugene Nygren, Duran Harris, Roy Warder and Mike Frison. Injured in the attack were Flynn, Kulage, Knapp, Giles and Burroughs. [4]

During the attack, Fr. Kilian could hear the moans and cries for help from soldiers who had been wounded. As he began to crawl out to provide aid and comfort, he was restrained by another officer, but only temporarily. "Those are my boys" he said, "I must go to them." And that is exactly what Fr. Kilian did, a very courageous act considering that nearly everyone else in the 92nd spent the entire night staring at the bottom of a foxhole.

It was after this attack that Fr. Kilian Dreiling, a Catholic chaplain, began to carry a .45 caliber automatic pistol. As he explained in a letter, "Nearly all of us do. We figure that one, live Catholic chaplain is worth more than forty dead japs..." [5]

The events of January 19 brought the war even closer to home for members of the 92nd. They had seen many men die before, but now they had suffered nine casualties from their own ranks. Many of the men were greatly disturbed by this event, and Fr. Kilian immediately began to console them. He also wrote heartfelt letters to all four of the deceased men's parents. In an act of compassion, he showed these letters to many of the men to help them come to grips with their own emotions.

Fr. Kilian would receive responses from many of the parents to whom he wrote these tender letters. He would save them all, telling himself that one day, when the pain of the war was softened by time, he would read them again. However, he later found that even after many years the pain would be re-awakened once again. One letter in particular, Fr. Kilian saved as being representative of the many he had received. The painful emotions that could only be felt by a parent who had just lost a son are clearly in evidence. Fr. Kilian would later read this next letter from the mother of Duran Harris at the first reunion of the 92nd evacuation hospital, 30 years after the war. Duran was killed during the infiltration of the 92nd's compound on January 19th.

"My dear Chaplain Dreiling: July 16th, 1945

"Your nice and much appreciated letter came a few days ago. I was more than pleased to receive it.

"Thanks <u>again</u> and <u>again</u>, for the lovely words you said about my son Duran. You know that mothers never tire of hearing good things about their children. It is nature. Also, I feel sure that you too, feel that all you said, about my dear son, had to be said.

"I feel very sure that if he could talk to us, he would have many, many good things to say about you, his chaplain (and how I wish I could hear him say them). These things mean so much to me, since I shall never again hear, or talk, or associate with him in the flesh. This last phase of his life seems so sacred to me; since I never saw him once he was inducted. I have still another son in Europe, whom I have never seen either, after being inducted in the Army. I have never seen either of my boys in uniform. And it is quite natural, for a mother, to want to see her sons, and admire them while they wear the grand old U.S.A. uniform. This is, I know, a touch of pride. It is of minor importance. Still we mothers feel that way.

"May God bless you and everyone like you, with more and more of His choicest blessings, and bring you and his comrades home, before much longer."

Unfortunately for Mrs. Harris, her sufferings were not over. She would later receive word that her second, and only living son was killed in action in Europe.

Soon after the 6th Army's landings at Lingayen, another chaplain was so impressed by Fr. Kilian's efforts that he felt compelled to write a letter to the Precious Blood Society in Carthagena, OH.

"... to let you know about the good work that Father Dreiling is doing over here. Besides his duties at the hospital he has given two or three missions to the men of the 41st Infantry Division. The mission in my regiment was a great success. The men were impressed not only by his eloquence but by his sympathetic and understanding attitude in helping them in their spiritual problems. His work in his own unit has the unstinted praise of every officer and enlisted man." [6]

This is high praise coming from a fellow Army chaplain. The Society of the Precious Blood had several chaplains in the Philippine Islands by this time. It was a rare, but joyous occasion when two C.PP.S. priests were able to get together during the war. Fr. Kilian's excitement is evident in this next note, sent back to Carthagena as he anticipates meeting both Fr. Aloys Selhorst and Fr. William Staudt.

"Father Staudt too just arrived and I also hope to see him shortly. I have hidden a gallon of native gin for our meeting. It is good, and the only good drink I have seen or tasted over here. If you hear of three PP.S. (Most Precious Blood) chaplains being court-martialed — well, have the members say the suffrages. None of this halfway business." [7]

We do not know how much "native gin," if any was left in Fr. Kilian's stash the next morning, but we do know that none of the three priests was arrested. Most likely their guardian angels worked overtime that evening.

They must have been terribly relieved to be able to swap stories and share their unbelievable experiences with the only other people who could possibly understand and appreciate them. And who better to unload your troubles upon than another Catholic chaplain from the same order? The daily strain of being the pillar that thousands of soldiers leaned upon would take a toll on the strongest individual. American GIs all over the world used the phrase, "Go tell it to the chaplain" for a reason. This was their euphemism for saying "I could care less about your problems." The chaplain didn't have a choice but to listen. It was his *job* to care about the soldiers' problems. Later in the war, Fr. Kilian would record some of these frustrations.

"This morning I left the hospital good and early. I was filled with the complaints of the boys. They started before breakfast, and every time I looked at one, he would start to complain about something — even my best men. Finally, I took the jeep and rode into the hills, to visit the six Sisters of Charity." [8]

Even the best chaplain is, after all, still human. Overall, Fr. Kilian Dreiling excelled at his "mission." In fact, he seemed to be energized by it. Throughout the rest of his life, he would never find a worthier cause, and he would use the lessons he had learned to teach others, almost until the day he died.

These photos of Fr. Kilian Dreiling were taken after his service in the Pacific. Note the Captain's bars on his shoulder and the service or campaign decorations above his left pocket. These photos were taken either before or during his service in post-WWII occupied Germany. Fr. Kilian retired from the U.S. Army with the rank of Major.

Enlisted men of the 92nd Evacuation Hospital pose outside thier tent during desert warfare training in California. Originally slated to join Patton's forces in North Africa, they were instead assigned to the 92nd. These men from "tent #17" are all Kentuckians, Hoosiers from Indiana or Buckeyes from Ohio. Front row (from left) "Jiggs" Griffith (IN), Joseph T. "Tommy" or "Smitty" Smith *author's father*, (KY), Guy McCants (IN),. Back row (from left) Bill Ahern *author's uncle*, (OH), Dubree (KY), unknown, Jim Reed (KY), Cecil Rhodes (KY), Mel Buscher (OH), Merle Wise (KY), Top of head (unknown), Parks (KY), unknown at far right.

Nurses from the 92nd pose after graduating from basic training, headed for the Pacific. The presence of female officers among their ranks gave the 92nd a different atmosphere than most Army companies. When fighting became too intense, the nurses would be moved to Australia, returning when things quieted down. However, they did endure bombings from Japanese planes and were otherwise exposed to the same hardships.

Nurse Peggy Bettmer cuddles two koala bear cubs in Australia. The 92nd trained for months in Australia for the upcoming invasion of the New Guinea Islands.

Nurses of the 92nd in their fatigues pose for the camera. Their unique, shared experiences and hardships forged lifelong friendships. From left, nurses Loomis, Betty Elder, Eugenia Rozbril, Betty Griffith, Phillips, unknown, Marion Larue.

Nurse Elenor Williams poses outside the "Pre-Op and Shock Ward" with the author's father, Joseph T. Smith. Note the bedpans and "ducks" (portable urinals) at right.

Fr. Kilian Dreiling, somewhere in the Pacific, poses outside his tent.

Two views of the log chapel constructed by the 92nd on Owi Island, 1944, inside (right) and front view (below).

Fr. Kilian poses in front of his tent chapel in the Philippines.

Fr. Kilian poses with enlisted man Bill Ahern (author's uncle) of the 92nd. 50 years later, the smiles of both men were just as warm as they were on the day this photo was taken.

Captain John Mihalek, one of the true leaders among the 92nd's officer corps. A former coal miner, Dr. Mihalek endeared himself to the enlisted men by championing their causes. On one occasion, Dr. Mihalek was "busted" from Major to Captain for defending some 92nd enlisted men in an Australian bar fight.

While stationed on Owi Island, the 92nd took care of the fighter and bomber crews of MacArthur's Fifth Air Force. From Owi, long-range B-24 Liberator bombers like this one could threaten the Philippine Islands. Friendships (and rivalries) developed between members of the 92nd and the flight crews like the men pictured here. (Owi Island was only 1.5 miles long and 1 mile wide.)

Members of the 92nd assemble for the presentation of a medal for bravery, given to Dr. Bill Baker. Baker battled strong ocean currents as he swam to rescue a downed aviator from a B-24 bomber that crashed into the sea upon take-off. The 92nd was fortunate to have such leaders. Their dress khaki uniforms were rarely worn while they were in the Pacific.

Comedian Bob Hope and his traveling troupe of entertainers treated the 92nd and the Fifth Air Force to a show on Owi Island. Bob Hope is seated at front (holding microphone). On his left are actresses Patty Thomas and Frances Langford. Comedian Jerry Colona is standing at the microphone.

Two Kentuckians, both from the city of Owensboro, "Tommy" Smith and Bob Brown, mug for the camera in front of a B-24 nicknamed "Art's Cart." This bomber's crew were veterans of many missions as evidenced by the number of bomb sillhouettes painted on the nose. The small white emblems indicate that the crew was credited with sinking five enemy ships.

The presence of dense jungle in the background indicates that this tent-chapel was probably located somewhere in the Philippine Islands. Enlisted man Kulage poses in front.

The church built by Chaplain Dreiling with the help of Filipinos at Caba, September 1945.

One of the many Japanese mountain guns which rained shells down upon American troops with devastating effect on Biak Island, New Guinea.

Japanese tanks knocked out by American tanks in a rare Pacific tank battle on Biak Island, New Guinea.

Chapter 12

The Search for a Brother

There was another C.PP.S. Chaplain in the Philippines who Fr. Kilian was even more anxious to meet. Fr. John Wilson was one of the first priests to enlist as a chaplain during WWII. He was taken prisoner by the Japanese along with the thousands of American soldiers that General MacArthur had been forced to leave behind in the Philippines. Fr. Wilson's story had been followed closely by all of the C.PP.S. priests in the early stages of the war. Once he became a POW they became gravely concerned for his safety as the Japanese allowed very little information to leak out of their prison camps. [1]

Fr. Wilson's story is quite remarkable and worthy of publication, but we will concern ourselves with those elements relevant to Fr. Kilian Dreiling's story. Fr. Kilian searched for Fr. Wilson so fervently that his search could be described as a quest. He would question anyone who might have information about Fr. Wilson's whereabouts or well being, and would follow up on any leads they might provide him. Fr. Kilian would even do things that others would consider irrational at best and crazy by most. He would drive through enemy-infested areas, braving sniper and artillery fire, always keeping his trusty jeep moving as fast as the primitive roads would allow, in the hope of reaching Fr. Wilson in time to help him.

Fr. Kilian sent a great deal of correspondence back to Carthagena informing them of his progress or lack thereof in finding Fr. Wilson. It seemed he was always just a little late, as the Japanese kept relocating their prisoners away from the advancing American Army. The fear that the Japs would tire of moving their prisoners around and simply massacre them was not unfounded. By now, the Americans had seen and heard evidence of the Japanese performing acts of unspeakable cruelty and barbarity, and believed them capable of almost anything. On February 1, 1945, Fr. Kilian writes,

"Fr. Wilson, whom I had hoped to see, as I passed, I visited his place, but most unfortunately he too had been removed. I spoke to priests who were with him only a few months ago when he was fine. He was not wounded, but my former fears have all but been confirmed." [2] Later, on Feb. 5, Fr. Kilian elaborates about his fears.

"I regret profoundly that the day has arrived when I must tell you that my earlier premonition has been verified. Last night in a heavy downpour of rain a batch of mail arrived. Among the letters was Chaplains' Letter No. 65, containing Father Vincent Nels' explanation why my cablegram was not sent: "The officials did not want to release the news of the torpedoing of the Japanese cargo ship carrying prisoners. There were practically no survivors." I had some rumor of this previously, but only after I arrived here was it confirmed. There is still the slim hope of "practically" in Father (Vincent) Nels' letter."

"After I arrived here, in the hope that Father (John) Wilson might be among the few left behind, I advanced for miles under fire of snipers and heavies to reach his former location, only to find the place abandoned and demolished. I could only let fall bitter tears and retreat slowly in silence with a prayer that he might still be among the "practically" few. I dread to think of our poor prisoners on the Islands of Japan. The Japs are the closest thing to mad animals that you can find. Father Provincial, in the near future you should get complete information. I have made arrangements to that effect." [3]

Fr. Kilian was not the only one searching for Fr. Wilson. C.PP.S. priest Fr. Aloys Selhorst, one of the two who helped Fr. Kilian finish off his "native gin," provides more detailed information about the condition of Fr. Wilson, as well as insight into the excellent work he was performing inside the prison camp. Fr. Selhorst's revelations about the Japanese atrocities help to explain why the American GIs began to perceive the Japanese soldiers as "animals." His comments about his admiration for the faith exhibited by the impoverished Filipino people are sentiments echoed by Fr. Kilian as well.

"In our hospital is a man who lived with Father John Wilson, in fact, he slept next to him. I asked him to write down everything he knew about Father Wilson. This he gladly did and presented it to me. For reasons of military security I may not send that letter. This much I can quote: "Father Wilson was one of the most lovable characters I knew during my prison days. To know him was to love him." An interesting sideline is that this party is now a convert to the Catholic Church, and is to be baptized this coming Sunday. We can be sure that the life, character and prayers of Father Wilson had much to do with this conversion."

"What happened here, I am sure, will be put down as one of the blackest episodes of history. It is impossible for the imagination to comprehend the diabolical and inhuman crimes by the Japs. To see soldiers shot, bayoneted, and blown to bits, is expected in war. And also modern warfare, to see civilians suffer from bombs, shells, and fire. But to hear story after story from civilians fortunate enough to survive, of seeing their entire family bayoneted, buried alive, their homes burned, without military reason, but purely hatred, staggers the imagination. In the hospital I see the horrible wounds that have been inflicted. These are the few that survive. Many others do not live to tell their story. I do not believe that I exaggerate when I say that some of the things that happened here would put Nero and Caligula to shame.

"It is edifying to see these people drink their overflowing cup of bitterness and sorrow with such great courage, calmness, and resignation. To illustrate I will mention one case. Visiting the patients in the hospital I met a Filipino youth who had aged quickly because of hunger and pain. On his chest were tattooed these words: 'Born to suffer.' On his one arm: 'Trust in God.' On the other 'God wills it.' In some places the words of Holy Scripture are literally fulfilled: 'Not a stone upon a stone shall remain.' With presumed permission, I am using some of my income to feed the hungry. I know of no greater need for charity. My health is good and work is plentiful... Father Dreiling just came in and I shall visit with him tonight." [4]

On April 11, Fr. Kilian writes that he has strong evidence suggesting that Fr. Wilson has been placed aboard a ship to be headed for Japan. He states, "From what I hear from our soldiers, I fervently hope that Father John never sees the shores of Japan."⁵ A letter sent by C.PP.S. Fr. Herbert Kramer on April 14, details how Fr. Kilian's hopes did not materialize.

"This week, through indirect channels, we have received some interesting side-lights on Father (Kilian) Dreiling, and also further clarification of his earlier messages about Father (John) Wilson. On September 7, 1944, a Jap ship carrying prisoners of war from the Philippines was sunk by our Navy. Only 82 of 700 were saved. Among the rescued were a number of soldiers who knew Father Wilson. One of them was his server. Father Dreiling it seems met some of these survivors and obtained from them the news he cabled to Father Provincial in September. That message has not arrived to this day."

"Father Wilson, together with two shiploads of prisoners was taken from this same Cabanatuan prison camp in September, 1944, en route to Japan both ships were sunk. Father Wilson, it seems then, must have been a survivor of this mishap, for we have word that he was in Japan and certified as a non-combatant as late as January, 1945."

Father John Wilson would prove to be amazingly resilient. He was also a remarkable man of faith who earned the respect not only of his fellow POWs but of his ruthless Japanese captors as well. Fr. Kilian would write that survivors of the Cabanatuan prison camp reported that Fr. Wilson should have "died a thousand deaths in as far as he was fearless, and defied the Japs, saying Mass when and where he pleased."⁷ This next, fascinating letter from an ex-P.O.W. who knew Fr. Wilson at camp Cabanatuan reveals great admiration for both Fr. Wilson and Fr. Dreiling. After being rescued by the American Rangers in one of the most daring raids in American history, he met Fr. Kilian Dreiling at the 92nd Evacuation Hospital. The ex-P.O.W., who was also a chaplain, wrote the following laudatory letter to the C.PP.S. Father Provincial.

"Until I have thanked you for kindness at the hands of Father Wilson and Father Dreiling, I have a debt unpaid. But even after thanking you, it will not be enough — only continued prayers at the altar will repay them. I was with Father Wilson for about one month at Cabanatuan after my arrival from Davao. At the time, I was a stranger in a strange land and he and (another priest) took good care of me. I was quite ill at the time and both of them looked after me, until they were taken from the camp to be transported to Japan. Father Wilson was doing excellent work, both physical and spiritual, and the men were in great admiration of him. Two days after I was rescued by the Rangers, I was taken to the hospital where Father Dreiling was stationed (the 92nd Evacuation Hospital). What an indefatigable worker. The section was quite "hot" at the time, and ambulances were rolling in twenty-four hours a day. When Father Dreiling slept, no one was able to find out. There were the Sacraments for our own, and prayers and consolation for all. His kindness to us prisoners of war brought tears to the eyes of all of us. May God bless and give you many priests of this standard! Our boys have too few chaplains, and I'm anxious to get back with them soon." [8]

Whether through the grace of God, the prayers of the Society of the Precious blood, or both, Fr. John Wilson would survive 3-1/2 years of captivity in Japanese prison camps and would return home to the U.S.A. after the war. News of his survival would bring joy to the heart of every C.PP.S. chaplain scattered throughout the world. *

Probably none of these priests was any more joyful than Fr. Kilian Dreiling. After failing in his efforts to locate Fr. Wilson, Fr. Kilian had despaired as he reluctantly faced the slim odds of Fr. Wilson's survival. Nevertheless, Fr. Kilian never gave up hope. An emotional man, it is hard to imagine him not shedding tears of joy upon hearing this unbelievable news. A brother who had been lost was now found!

There are many similarities between Fr. John Wilson and Fr. Kilian

---

* Fr. John Wilson would go on to live a full life in the service of his order. In 1947 he would be named "Vicar Provincial," overseeing the C.PP.S. society's new and ambitious South American missionary initiative. One reason given for his selection by Fr. Marling was to "give voice from the start to the one who must ultimately guide the new establishment." The second reason provides insight into the level of respect and admiration that the C.PP.S. society held for Fr. Wilson.

"I know that many will think, as we have thought, that Father Wilson was saved from peril (initial bombing of the Philippine Islands, Coregidor, the Death March, deportation across jeopardous seas and imprisonment in Japan) and brought almost miraculously through trial and sorrow for a great purpose." [9]

Dreiling. Both were men of deep faith who became great, inspirational leaders as their respective situations required. Both were pillars of strength, whose examples of selfless behavior and compassion would inspire thousands. Indeed, many conversions can be attributed to both men. The prayer of St. Francis of Assisi was truly fulfilled through these two men. "Where there was doubt... (they provided) faith, where there was despair... hope, where there was darkness... light, and where there was sadness... joy!"

One of the purposes for including this chapter about Fr. Kilian's quest to find Fr. Wilson, was to point out that while Fr. Kilian was a rare man, even among chaplains, he was not alone. Indeed, there were many great men who volunteered to place themselves in harm's way in order to bring badly needed spiritual direction and comfort to young men who faced death almost daily. Many of these men were from Fr. Kilian's own order, the C.PP.S. Society, and were similarly devoted to their cause. While their stories may never be told to a wide audience, they were truly great men. Fr. Kilian's story speaks for them all.

Chapter 13

The 92nd's Finest Hour

The story of the daring raid by members of the 6th U.S. Rangers to free over 500 American prisoners from camp Cabanatuan on the Philippine island of Luzon was front page news in early February of 1945. Many of the American survivors of the "Bataan Death March" had spent years at this infamous camp, enduring unspeakable cruelties at the hands of their captors. A great many Americans did not survive this hell, falling victim to diseases like dysentery, malaria, to starvation and torture. About 2300 prisoners were buried at the camp.

General Douglas MacArthur had personally ordered the Cabanatuan rescue mission, and he badly wanted it to succeed. On January 30th, a force of 121 U.S. Rangers, supported by 286 Filipino Guerrillas, attacked the Japanese guards at Cabanatuan prison camp on Luzon, P.I. This carefully planned and brilliantly coordinated attack was made possible through excellent intelligence provided by Filipino Scouts and civilians. An entire Japanese division, supported by tanks was nearby, so the attacking force had to move in and out swiftly. Road blocks were set up on roads leading into Cabanatuan to prevent Japanese reinforcements from descending upon the rescuers. [1]

The spectacular success of this rescue operation is well known to historians who have studied the American Pacific campaign. Led by Lieutenant Colonel Henry A. Mucci, the Rangers liberated 513 American, Dutch and British POWs while killing 223 Japanese soldiers at the prison camp and hundreds more while fending off counter-attacks. American Ranger casualties included 27 killed and two wounded. All of the Rangers who participated were decorated for this operation, which is still the most successful rescue mission in the history of the U.S. armed forces.

Less well-known however, is the critical role that the 92nd Evacuation Hospital played in providing immediate, badly needed hospital care to the gaunt and emaciated prisoners. On the morning before the raid, the 92nd was given orders from Brigadier General William A. Hagins, 6th Army Surgeon to "Pack up and get down to Guimba by this afternoon. Set up and be ready to take patients immediately." [1]

The town of Guimba was 60 miles away from where the 92nd had been stationed. By now, they were a veteran unit, capable of promptly executing the swift move of their entire several hundred-bed hospital to within a short few miles of U.S. forward infantry elements. Rumors were rampant as to where the 92nd was headed and for what purpose. The journey itself was nerve-wracking as they drove past rice paddies that had been battlefields less than 24 hours earlier. They were well aware that Japanese soldiers were not far away, and it was easy to imagine snipers behind every haystack.

After arriving at Guimba, they selected the town's elementary school as the best site for the hospital. By the end of the first evening, they had power, a supply room, operating room, laboratory and wards with sheeted cots. Now they were ready, but extremely anxious.

Before Lt. Colonel Mucci and his Rangers made their daring raid however, they first quietly and stealthily showed up at the 92nd Hospital for a short rest. During this period, Lt. Colonel Mucci asked Fr. Kilian to hear the confessions of his Catholic soldiers before undertaking this high-risk operation.

Earlier in the afternoon the 92nd had been visited by an American officer with a reconnaissance patrol. The officer asked them, "What the hell outfit are you with?" Upon hearing that they were the 92nd Evacuation Hospital, the officer asked, "Do you know that you are 75 miles ahead of the infantry and that not too far down the road about 30 or 40 miles there is a huge contingent of the Japanese Army?" [2]

Many years later, Dr. Colvin recorded his reaction to hearing this unnerving comment. "After my adam's apple returned from where it had sunk into my stomach — I asked him what could be done. He replied, "There are about 500 Philippine Guerrillas in the adjacent town who can possibly help you." That evening, the guerrillas arrived and set up a perimeter around the camp together with some of our men. I was bravely kneeling down in the holes we had dug when all of a sudden the guerrilla captain, upon hearing a noise, jumped out of the trench and yelled, "You goddammed Jap — come on we are not afraid of you!" From almost my prone position I was tempted to say, "Speak for yourself, John." Some rifle shots were heard, and in the early morning we discovered two dead bodies — both cows!" [2]

After a rather sleepless night, the trucks began to arrive around noon of the next day. They had been sent out to meet the caravan of prisoners, half being hauled in native caribou carts, half staggering in on foot after a debilitating 22 mile hike. This would be a day that all of the members of the 92nd would never forget. The returning prisoners were jubilant, and their soaring spirits would lift the hearts of the members of the 92nd as well. Emotions were running high as the joy of welcoming these men back to a world of freedom, dignity and plenty was balanced by the sadness and realization that these men had just suffered a hell on earth. Years later, many would consider this event one of the greatest moments of their lives. They were grateful to have had the opportunity to offer assistance to men who had sacrificed so much for their countrymen. Dr. Colvin expressed his feelings after this event.

"Nothing ever occurred again to give me that surge of patriotism, accomplishment or joy when I first sighted the trucks bringing them (the American POW's) into our camp. I remember their first meal, the look of contentment and pleasure the food gave them." [2]

One of the first faces that many of the prisoners saw at the hospital was Fr. Kilian Dreiling. He recalled how difficult it was to have to tell the emaciated men, who longed to fill their bellies, that they could only eat the rich food in small portions...for now. It was Kilian's kindness and boundless energy that so moved one former POW that he was compelled to write the Father Provincial of the C.PP.S. order the heartfelt thank you letter mentioned in the previous chapter.

After seeing to the welfare of the freed POWs, Fr. Kilian could wait no longer for news of Fr. John Wilson. Two days after the camp was freed, Fr. Kilian and a small recon patrol embarked down the unguarded road back to camp Cabanatuan to see if he could find evidence of Fr. Wilson's recent presence, or perhaps with luck, Fr. Wilson himself. Accompanied by two officers and three ex-POW's, Fr. Kilian travelled through a non-secured area while dodging Japanese sniper and heavy artillery fire. Fr. Kilian tells of this harrowing trip in his own notes from Sept. 7, 1944.

"For miles we were under shell fire. One mountain gun let go and the shell went over our heads. Snipers are everywhere."

They returned with the camp hospital's medical records, but with little new information about Fr. Wilson's whereabouts. By now, the men of the 92nd were used to their chaplain's willingness to take risks in situations where he felt he could make a positive difference. It was with good reason that they continually worried about his safety.

Back in the United States, the news of the daring Cabanatuan rescue provided another morale boost. Within days of the rescue, Gen. MacArthur himself, never one to miss a photo opportunity visited the 92nd Evacuation Hospital compound. Many reporters were there to cover the event, and several family members of 92nd men were thrilled to find photographs of their loved ones featured back home in the local papers.

Fr. Kilian recorded that on three separate occasions, he met with General MacArthur. The condition of the prisoners would certainly have been one of the primary topics of their conversations. In addition, Fr. Kilian was one of only three members of the 92nd who had actually seen the infamous camp Cabanatuan. Therefore, he would have certainly given MacArthur his first-hand account of the tragic conditions that the American POWs had been exposed to, and all of the graves that he had witnessed. Here is what Fr. Kilian wrote in his letter back to his Fr. Provincial.

"The sight of the camp was sickening. You never saw such a rat-hole. Eight would sleep next to one another and whenever one would turn, all had to turn. About 2300 prisoners who had died of starvation are buried there. Only one grave was dug each day, and as many as forty were buried in some graves. One Catholic soldier, who had obtained food from the natives, was forced to dig his own grave, one foot deep, and lie in it. He was shot, because he refused to have his eyes blinded, and as long as one looks a Jap in the face he can't kill him. So, a Jap officer, from afar, threw a dagger into him and in that way he came to his tragic end." [3]

It is almost certain that Fr. Kilian sought General MacArthur's assistance in his efforts to locate Fr. Wilson. This would explain Kilian's comments back to Fr. Provincial that, "In the future, you can expect complete information. I have made arrangements to that effect."[4] This is extremely definitive language for a Captain in the U.S. Army. It later became apparent that Fr. Kilian had been able to develop something of a rapport with MacArthur, who felt a strong connection to the troops he had left behind. In 1985, Fr. Kilian Dreiling was asked to speak at a graveside memorial service for Douglas MacArthur, who had been very complimentary of the 92nd for its care of the Cabanatuan prisoners.

Sgt. Joe Smith provides another very interesting account of General MacArthur's visit to the 92nd Evacuation Hospital.

"MacArthur walked into my ward and stood directly in front of the Colonel who had been the senior-most American officer in the prison camp. The Colonel looked up at MacArthur and said, "Sit down. If you think I'm gonna' stand up and salute you, you S.O.B. you're crazy!" [5]

General MacArthur then proceeded to sit down and carry on a quiet conversation with the colonel, apparently willing to forgive the insubordination in light of the terrible ordeal he had faced (and that MacArthur had escaped).

The 92nd's mission to offer aid and comfort to the Cabanatuan POW's was at the same time, well executed and perilous. Tensions and emotions had run extremely high, and even 50 years later, these memories were still vivid for most of the participants. Fr. Kilian and his comrades had every reason to be proud of their accomplishments.

However, the costs of war do not end when the enemy surrenders and the soldiers go home. Many members of the 92nd , like so many other soldiers, sailors and airmen, would be haunted by visions of what they had seen for years to come. Fr. Kilian, having seen more than his share of horror, would suffer greatly for the rest of his life. 50

years later, he would awake from a startling nightmare that had been fueled by his Cabanatuan experiences. He immediately took pen in hand and wrote the following story.

"Hopefully"

Perhaps, yes perhaps by committing my memories to concrete paper or carving them on a stone tablet like the Ten Commandments, my soul will find rest, my mind respite.

Only last night I awoke with a fearful start, drenched in a cold sweat from head to foot. True, the culprit was only an imitation of the historical past, nevertheless, the effect, mental and physical, was even more devastating. In time of actual battle, one is more apt to be preoccupied with survival or outside concerns like the safety of one's comrades etc. In a dream one seems to concentrate on one particular, totally exaggerated, even an impossible and ridiculous element.

What occasioned this incident goes back nearly fifty years. During WWII, Bishop Marling, our superior, kept me well informed as to the possible whereabouts of our Father Wilson (chaplain) during his captivity in the Southwest Pacific. Most often, his was sheer speculation. Other times he was right on target but late. The latter was the case when we liberated the prisoners of Cabanatuan Luzon, P.I. He was right on target, true, but two months late. Johnnie was, indeed, in the infamous camp for a number of years, but had now left for Japan two months before our arrival. We, the 92nd Evacuation Hospital, set up camp in a little village, Guimba, twenty miles inside enemy territory, precisely to receive the prisoners, so we learned later. However, because the movement was Top Secret stuff, much confusion kept us in suspense.

For example, without foreknowledge or forewarning, the famous Rangers moved in on us in absolute stealth, for which they have a reputation, and for which purpose they are trained. The CO of the unit searched for me immediately and begged that I have confessions and Mass for his unit. That over, and a quick evening meal after Mass, and they were off as quietly and mysteriously as they moved in on us. Like a corps of silent ghosts they pushed onward, under cover of darkness to reach the prison camp by early morning. In a total surprise attack they overpowered the unsuspecting Japanese guards, and in less than eight minutes they completely emptied the camp and were fast on their way to our hospital. By late afternoon some 500 prisoners draggled into our perimeter. Some still walked with discipline, others hobbled hesitatingly, while still others leaned heavily on a buddy or a kind native Samaritan. Not a few arrived on ox-carts, drawn by caribou. All understandably were emaciated and looked like lost and long forgotten souls back from purgatory, but now exceedingly happy! Unfortunately, more and more had to be restrained or guarded. The sudden release was too much.

As an ever-obliging chaplain, it became my duty to stand at the head of the chow line and ever so discreetly repeat over and over, "Soldier, for now just a little, just a little, but you may come back as often as you wish. If you eat too fast or too much you will get deadly sick." It was a touchy task. In their mental confusion they might resent my advice or misconstrue my intent.

The day following, a convoy headed for the camp to retrieve buried records, sacred diaries, official information of all sorts. My jeep was the third to enter the compound. It was a venturesome experience indeed.

But truly, it was the getting there that made the day historical. As we came near the village of Cabanatuan, we came upon a battlefield strewn with dead bodies, the result of a previous day-long and furious battle. Typically, the convoy veered neither to the right nor to the left. We were forced to drive over bodies all the way. I threw my jeep into low gear, four wheel drive, closed my eyes and blindly forged onward. The "never-to-die impact" was not due to the many, many dead bodies (we had had that in New Guinea many times over), but in driving over bodies. I could feel the back wheels come down to earth with a sickening thump. In my bad dream last night every dead body was a mountain that led to a 400-foot cliff. As my back wheels tumbled over the cliff with a thunderous thump, I found myself floating in an ocean of human blood. But — even worse was the <u>actual</u> encounter, between the village and the prison camp, of truckloads of enemy soldiers. Because they were completely encircled and had no way of escaping, all systematically committed "hara-kiri."

There were countless, mutilated bodies in and around every truck. Each truck had between 40 and 60 soldiers. Naturally, human blood ran everywhere and I heard every drop of blood wail, "War is hell!"

It was after the second tumble over the cliff in my dream, that I awoke to the frightfully sobering thought, as I now focused my eyes on my lighted shrine of Jesus in the corner of my bedroom. I came to note most vividly and instantly the tremendously striking contrast, the comfortingly striking thought, yes, the loving contrast: Jesus too shed his precious blood, but not out of hate, or revenge or evil gain, or lust for insane power, but out of pure, infinite love and compassion for all mankind- friend and enemy alike. Yes, he shed his Precious Blood not to destroy but to mend, not to mutilate but to heal, not to condemn but to pardon.

Human blood seems most often to be the price, the medium of exchange, in defeat over victory, in loss over gain, in greed over power, revenge, and retaliation. Divine blood too seems to be the medium of exchange, the price but always for holy gain, a Samaritan healing and a divine reconciliation.

Yes, divine blood, the blood of Jesus is the ever-ultimate manifestation, the everlasting expression, the glorious and eternal reflection of the very essence of Christianity. "Greater love than this no one has than to shed one's life for one's friends."

Chapter 14

Gathering the "Scattered Flock"

Fr. Kilian Dreiling was a complex man, driven by emotion and passion. Perhaps the emotion he could least ignore, was his strong sense of compassion. Whenever he encountered the poor, the sick, the disheartened or the dying, he felt compelled to do something to alleviate their pain.

One group of people who touched his heart was the many displaced and persecuted religious personnel encountered frequently by the 92nd. This was especially true for the nuns who Fr. Kilian affectionately referred to as "blackbirds" because of the black habits they wore. The Japanese Army had no sympathy for the many missionaries and local religious that they encountered during their conquest of the overwhelmingly Catholic Philippines. Strong religious leaders were considered a threat and many were persecuted, imprisoned, tortured and killed. Saying Mass openly was indeed, very dangerous.

Many of the priests and nuns had gone into hiding in the mountains. Fr. Kilian would enlist as much support from the 92nd as he could muster in order to offer them aid and comfort. On April 11th, 1945, Fr. Kilian wrote the following in a letter to his order.

"Everywhere the good kind sisters continue to show up. Truthfully, they are like a scattered flock of geese. Two are found here, another four there, and sometimes just one at a place. Daily we are awaiting the arrival of about fifty more who are heroically climbing the mountains to escape the Japs. Their ultimate fate is anybody's guess. We hope that the shrewd guerrillas will guide them through the passes. It has happened before. Nearly all the Sisters are Belgian. For they have done a marvelous job in a nearby town looking after the wounded soldiers and guerrillas. In fact, their work has received so much praise that they are completely supplied by our medical department. Priests too continue to roam about the country aimlessly, their churches destroyed, their flocks scattered."[1]

Fr. Kilian wrote several stories about these brave individuals and the unshakeable faith and courage that sustained them. The following story about a group of German Catholic nuns that Fr. Kilian encountered is both remarkable and heartwarming. After fleeing persecution in Hitler's Nazi Germany, these poor Sisters fled to the Philippine Island of Luzon, directly in the path of the Japanese Army.

"A Belated X-Mas Present"

Tarlac, Luzon, P.I., is located some 30 to 40 miles north of Manila. It, like most cities on the island, sits in the valley that runs all the way from Manila to the northern extremity of Luzon. Were one to count the inhabitants alone, it might correctly be called a city, but were one to consider the limited geographic space, it were better to be called a village. If we consider its fate during WWII it might more correctly be called historic.

During the siege of Manila and Tarlac, our hospital, the 92nd Evac Hospital, was located in Guimba, some twenty miles still further north. Our purpose there was to eventually receive over 500 military prisoners from the infamous prison camp of Cabanatuan. From the beginning, our mission was a top-secret matter. In fact, not even we, the members of the 92nd, knew exactly where we were going or why. A rude awakening however, came presently and with hurricane force. Now completely surrounded by the enemy, our casualties mounted rapidly. The famous rangers silently sneaked in on us, and after attending Mass and eating chow, left just as quietly. Tomorrow they would bring over 500 prisoners to our hospital for reconditioning. However, this also alerted the enemy into action. They took the offensive, at least for a few days.

It was at this time that we ran short on oxygen. My new CO came to me and asked, "Would you join our supply officer in search of oxygen? We are running dangerously short." I readily agreed, naturally.

As we left the perimeter and drove through the village, one could hear bullets hit in all directions. We inquired of the natives the shortest distance to Tarlac, for it was there that we might find oxygen we were told. They advised us to go through the rice paddies. Unfortunately, we did much to our regrets. We broke down one rice paddy wall after another, only to run into another and another, and still another. It was work, and it delayed us considerably. Eventually, we found the depot and secured our oxygen.

While loading my trailer with oxygen tubes, I seemed to smell freshly baked bread. I asked the MP if my nose served me right, and he assured me that the Army bakery was only two blocks to the right. We drove over and again I asked the MP what chances we had of begging a few slices of fresh bread. He in turn, called a corporal and I made my third time request. When he recalled our unit he said, "Boys, not only a slice but two fresh loaves, one for each of you." We thanked him profusely. However, as we sat in the jeep eating the good bread, the whole of Tarlac suddenly burst into flames, and before our very eyes. It erupted from a hundred points, and because the homes were mostly constructed out of bamboo poles and grass roofs, it vanished in less than an hour. Shortly, there was nothing left except black charcoal.

Strangely enough however, to the south of the village still stood a huge church, plus a few more hardy structures. These miraculously survived and we naturally wondered why. But our mission was to get the much-needed oxygen, so we returned with the greatest haste.

Toward noon the next day, the supply officer came to me and said, "Padre, don't you think that we should return to Tarlac to see if there are missionary sisters in need of food or medicine?" It was agreed that after lunch we would return to Tarlac. In broad daylight, the city sprawled out before us, black as Satan's soul. And on the far end still stood the buildings totally and visibly intact. We crossed over, and once there, I approached the building- most like usual convents. I knocked and waited, not knowing what exactly to expect. After a long silence, the front door opened ever so slightly, and a faint voice said, "Yes!" It was Reverend Mother herself answering in greatest visible apprehension. I promptly assured her that I was a Catholic chaplain, and that we were there to bring food and medicine. I naturally spoke to her in German and with that came reassurance. In her excitement she turned and literally yelled, "Swesters, kumt doch se sind doth frenude!" (Sisters, hurry, come they are friends).

While the Lt. And the sister carried in the food and medicine, I talked to Reverend Mother. She told me of the terrible fright they had experienced, how she had sent eight of the sisters into the mountains while eight remained in the convent. Their thinking she said, was that if they get killed in the mountains, we here may survive, or if we get killed, they hopefully would survive. (I learned much later that all survived). Finally, I said, "But Reverend Mother, what accounts for the fact that your church and school and convent still stand?" With an air of infinite relief, she told her story.

She said, "Father, when Tarlac began to burn we full well knew the plan of the Japanese, 'scorch the earth.' Our first thought was the church and the sacred hosts. We rushed to church and consumed all but eight hosts. These we brought into our convent, placed them on this table and prayed that God preserve our church and school and convent, and our sisters in the mountains. Suddenly, there was a knock at the door. Instinctively, we decided that that was the last of us. You see, we had heard much of the atrocities of the enemy. We consumed all but one host before I answered the door. By now, the knock had been repeated, but when I fearfully opened the door, I saw standing on our porchway, a huge Japanese officer. In a stern voice he asked, "You are Catholic missionary sisters?" I answered ever so weakly, "Yes officer, we are German Catholic missionary Sisters. We were driven out of Germany by Hitler." With a relaxed composure now, he said with a faint smile, "Sister, do not worry about your buildings. I too am a Catholic. Your church and convent will not burn down. I have charge of the burning of this section and I will not permit it to be burned down, ever. Now sister, I must be about my business."

He walked a few feet, turned around and with great satisfaction said, "Sister, I am a St. Francis Catholic." (Recall that St. Francis Xavier converted many, many Japanese 500 years before, namely in the 16th century. This officer was a direct descendant.) With great relief I closed the convent door."

But now a third time he knocked at the door. In a most friendly manner he said, "And sister, since X-Mas is so near, I bring you a X-Mas gift from St. Francis: Accept as an X-mas gift your church, your school and your convent, and hopefully all your sisters in the mountains." With that he departed and we never saw him again. I said, "Mother, you should in gratitude change the name of your convent to Merry X-mas." This they did. "And more" I said, "Mother, let the spirit in this convent be one of hope, cheerfulness and joy." And again she said, "Father, we will." We left and we never saw them again.

Fr. Kilian would later send this story to friends and family as a X-mas letter. It seemed he had the gift of searching through his rich "treasure house" of memories for a story, which was appropriate for the moment. By repeatedly going out of his way, or "above and beyond" his duty to help others, Fr. Kilian repeatedly exposed himself to situations that became excellent material for his stories. In the words of some, he went "looking for trouble," and he usually found it.

The practice of seeking out the local priests and nuns and offering assistance had by now, become Standard Operating Procedure for the members of the 92nd. This explains the supply officer's (Ed Gray's) comment, "Padre, don't you think we should return to Tarlac to see if there are missionary sisters in need of food or medicine?" Fr. Kilian had helped create a culture, an "esprit de corps" that encouraged the staff to go beyond caring for the patients who happened to be brought into the 92nd Evacuation Hospital. By now, they were also pro-actively seeking out those who needed assistance, and this practice had become "ordinary." This was a special unit with a rare spiritual leader. Only thirty years later, at their first reunion, would they fully appreciate how truly special the 92nd was.

At this point in the conquest of the Philippines during March and April of 1945, the 92nd was stationed in a village called Agoo La Union. The Americans had recently liberated Manila, the largest city in the Philippine Islands. Agoo was one half mile from the coast above San Fabian.

The Americans were driving on the strategic city of Baguio in the northern Philippines. Baguio had been the "summer capital" of the Philippine government, and was now the last major bastion of resistance for the Japanese Army. The Japanese were fighting furiously in a futile attempt to delay the inevitable American victory. The mountainous terrain made progress slow for the American troops. The city of Baguio took a terrible beating during this time, as the Americans bombed the Japanese outpost relentlessly. This resulted in the creation of hundreds of Philippine refugees, who clogged the narrow roads leading from Baguio, and complicated the efforts of the American troops moving toward the city.

During this period, Fr. Kilian was doing his best to help the refugees by bringing them as much food and medicine as possible. Fr. Kilian was often moved by the simple faith of the Filipino people, who persevered despite their hardships. This next story was written by Fr. Kilian some 35 years later, as he looked back fondly upon an experience he had with a Belgian Catholic Nun who risked her life in order to minister to these refugees.

"Mother Donata"

During the actual bombing of Baguio, P.I. in 1945, countless missionary sisters, priests and lay people naturally fled the city. There was nowhere to go except down because the city sits on the knoll of the highest mountain in the area. The shortest and fastest escape was to take to the mountain trail still in the hands of the enemy. In all, there must have been between 500 and 700 refugees. The trail ziz-zagged down the mountain through enemy territory and treacherous terrain, and eventually came out into a beautiful valley and the village, Tubao. From the air, the tiny village looked like a peaceful, sleepy hollow, totally protected on all sides by mountainous skyscrapers. The valley was exceedingly fertile and naturally productive. In the center stood a huge metal church of early Spanish vintage. The church was surrounded by humble homes and even humbler people. Belgian Sisters and priests cared for the spiritual welfare of the natives from time immemorial. The rectory was quickly requisitioned and became the center of much activity. The sisters' convent became the center shelter for all and the school was used for housing refugees. The same Belgian Sisters had charge of Agoo, some seven miles from Tubao, where we, the 92nd Evac Hospital were located. Agoo was for a number of years, the headquarters of the enemy for that northern area. Tubao could only be reached by a circuitous and dangerous pass, still a safe terrain of the Japanese army. To bring food to the encircled "dorf," I had to drive carefully and cautiously, keep an eye on every rock or coconut in the hope of catching sight of a sniper and quickly get out of his reach. For fully a week I evaded the snipers and enemy soldiers in and around the difficult pass.

But the day came when calamity reigned in the peaceful valley. Mother Donata, a simple, holy nun, on her own, had gone up the trail looking for the caravan in the hope of leading them safely to the valley. Mother Donata had not yet returned. She was overdue by nearly two days. When I next returned to Tubao, sisters, priests and natives swarmed around my jeep like hungry bees. All talked at the same time and loudly. "Mother Donata and her Bernard have not returned." Already, it was firmly concluded, "Mother Donata and her St. Bernard were either captured by the enemy soldiers or fell afoul of a wild animal." Dusk moved in rapidly in the valley encircled by high mountains, and I had to return to my base, again through the hazardous pass.

Determined not to forsake the good natives, I returned as usual the next afternoon to find Mother Donata drawing water with a 15-foot bamboo pole. When I approached her, she dropped the bucket down the well and with an impish smile, awaited my word. With mixed feelings, joy at seeing her safe, and slightly angry that she exposed the village to fear and anxiety, I rather curtly said, "Mother, don't you ever again go out into the mountains without protection. Ask for soldiers and the army will gladly give them to you. But remember Mother, the mountains are still infested with enemy soldiers and you are in great danger of being captured and ruthlessly killed." She listened patiently, much like the little altar boys back home, but finally reached down, took the crucifix of her rosary, held it up to my face and ever so sweetly said, "Fadder, when God is mit mere no danger...not afraid at all-I!" Her faith was so sincere, so simple, so true, that without another further thought I simply said, "Mother, with a faith like that I even urge you and Bernard to follow the trail. Perhaps this time you will find the caravan and ultimately lead them happily home to the valley." Well, she did just that the following day, found the train of refugees, and led them down into the valley-home. I arrived just in time to see the last of the caravan emerge from the jungle. In fact, I came just in time to carry Mother Petra out of the last of the jungle to the local convent. Mother Petra had lost a leg during the bombing and had to be carried all the way. (All the sisters in the U.S. had pitched in and bought her an artificial leg). Most fortunately, the mess Sgt. Gave me a mattress cover full of bread, plus many other eatable which the sisters kindly shared with all.

Our next problem-the flies! They actually darkened the sun and swarmed through the air like snowflakes in a blizzard. The military quickly took over, sprayed the area, and within hours, there was scarcely a fly within miles.

In due time, I took time to go and see Mother Donata. I thanked her for her great and heroic act of charity towards all. She again listened most attentively, bowed her head humbly, and ever so meekly replied, "Fadder, thank you but God, HE did...no way find them without him." Then, with an angelic smile, and I thought with an impish grin, she said as she patted her St. Bernard, "Fadder, he too do," pointing with her index finger and thumb, "just so little."

In conclusion, I offered her a proposition that later I offered to Sr. Eunice. Said I, "Mother, would you consider taking over this war with the help of the good Lord and Bernard, and let us all go home?" Her reply was prompt and playful. "Ha Fadder, one enemy soldier, Bernard and I can conquer, but a whole big army we no can do... unless God will it."

As I returned once more to my unit late at night, I could only repeat, "If only I had the faith of Mother Donata, I would move every mountain between Agoo and Tubao and the enemy as well. Well, I did not move the mountains, but the Lord eventually made the pass as safe as my tent. In other words, the good Lord did for me what indeed he did for Mother Donata, only in His own way and His own time.

Although his peers recognized Fr. Kilian as an intellectual and a theologian, he always felt that he learned more through the humble and simple faith of special individuals, like Mother Donata. Fr. Kilian's own faith was strengthened by such encounters, and he would in turn, strengthen many others by his own demonstration of faith. By recording the life experiences that he cherished most, beautiful stories like that of the simple little Belgian nun live on.

By this time, Fr. Kilian had earned something of a reputation among the U.S. Army and the local Filippinos for his efforts in aiding the local clergy and their scattered parishioners. Fr. William Staudt, another C.PP.S. priest assigned to the Philippines, reports with admiration about Fr. Kilian's efforts.

"I find it difficult to compete with Father Dreiling. I saw him about three weeks ago and plan to make another trip sometime next week. He is well and is looking just the same. He is to be commended for his help to the sisters and local clergy. Everyone has only praise for his work." [2]

In a letter home to his fellow priests, Fr. Kilian explains how his "hands-on" approach to helping the locals takes many by surprise.

"This morning I put the finishing touches to the roof of their house (six Sisters of Charity). The windows are still wide open. They do not even have money to buy the small rations obtainable from our government. They can't understand the American priests. Until we came over here and worked with our hands as well as our heads, no priest had ever laid hands to anything but books. At first we were pitied, looked upon as slightly simple. Now most of the priests (the locals) are ashamed to look at us. The example of our Catholic boys has taken the pride out of them. I work with five secular priests and they are the grandest men I ever met." [3]

Chapter 15

Peace at Last

As the campaign in the Philippines wound down, every American serviceman knew what was next on the agenda: The long-awaited and much-feared invasion of the Japanese islands themselves.

There was great cause for concern. The American soldiers had seen firsthand how fiercely the Japanese had defended even the tiny islands that had fallen to the American juggernaut one by one. Indeed, in most cases the Japanese had fought to the very last man. How many American lives would now be sacrificed in this last-ditch effort to bring the once mighty and fiercely proud Japanese people to their knees?

Most of the men and women of the 92nd by now considered themselves fortunate to have survived the war up to this point. However, they did not like their odds of survival in a bloody, house-to-house struggle on the Japanese homeland, one of the most densely populated places on earth. All hoped that the Japanese would see the hopelessness of their situation and simply surrender. However, nothing they had witnessed so far indicated that this was likely.

With the morale and welfare of the soldiers always at the forefront of Fr. Kilian's mind, he took advantage of this period of relative inactivity to provide an opportunity for them to blow off a little steam.

On June 24th he wrote, "Daily we are waiting for a better turn of events. The unusual number of surrenders has created new interest in our war. Perhaps the near future will see an end to it.

"I am kept busy...and many things to look after. Last Saturday night for example, I arranged a dance for the boys. I was there from the start to the finish. It was a big success, and the boys behaved well.

As usual, there were exceptions. A little liquor can produce much harm. But it serves a good purpose too. For it loosens the tongues of the men, and they come confessing their transgressions.

"Last Sunday, the new colonel, who is acting as our commanding officer, attended my Mass. He had to listen to me as I went after the men for their wrongdoing. I am told that the sermon brought about the closing of several houses. The colonel was impressed and made some complimentary remarks. He is a Southern Baptist." [1]

By this time, Fr. Kilian had earned enough "points" to warrant something that every soldier dreamed of, "stateside leave!" However, Fr. Kilian could not bear to leave his comrades at this critical time. He explains his rationale in the same June 24 letter.

"The opportunity will come to me to go home next month. I am first on the list. But I am going to turn it down. The very thought of seeing the States again is like heaven, but if I leave now I shall not be back in time and the men will be gone on a new push. So, I suppose I shall just stick it out for the duration. May God Bless you all." [2]

Less than two months later, the first of two atomic bombs would fall on Japan. News of the awesome new weapon brought hope to the American soldiers who were staging for the invasion of Japan. On August 14, Japan sued for Peace and August 15 became "Victory Day in Japan" or "V-J Day."

When news of the Japanese surrender reached the 92nd, everyone rushed to the mess tent to find out if this latest rumor was real. In the mad dash, one soldier tripped over a tent rope and broke his leg. [3] What they heard was almost unbelievable. The news was real! They truly were going home! Celebrations broke out immediately as hidden "stashes" of alcohol appeared out of nowhere. Fr. Kilian celebrated Mass in the chapel at the S.V.D. Seminary at 10:00 AM for all the departed. According to Fr. Kilian, "The chapel was stacked to capacity as the Filipinos sang movingly and lovingly throughout Mass." [4]

For almost four years, the members of the 92nd had endured exhaustive training, nauseating sea voyages, bombings and strafings, and one monotonous campaign after another. They had watched thousands of young men die far from their homes and their families, and they had all grown older and wiser. There were no longer any "boys" or "girls" among their ranks, just men and women who had become like family to each other. Many had either found or renewed their faith because of the efforts of Fr. Kilian Dreiling, and his effect upon them would be life long. Almost to a man or woman, the veterans of the 92nd would agree that the tall, passionate and engaging chaplain who joined them at Hollandia, New Guinea, had been the group's heart and its soul.

On September 2, they listened to the Japanese surrender ceremonies broadcast live from the deck of the battleship U.S.S. Missouri. However, the 92nd would soon receive some disheartening news. While most of the U.S. soldiers were being mustered out of the service, the 92nd had one more "campaign" to endure. On October 1st, they would board yet another ship, the "James O'Hara," and sail for one final destination before they could go home. This time they were headed for Nagoya, Japan to set up an occupation hospital. In spite of a great deal of complaining, they accomplished this last task together in their customary, professional fashion. Fr. Kilian however, would not make this last voyage with the 92nd.

Now that the war was truly over, Fr. Kilian chose to exercise the 30 days of stateside leave that he had earned. He would be one of the very first to reach home. We know that he spent August 14, the day the Japanese asked for surrender terms, with fellow C.PP.S. chaplain and good friend, Fr. Aloys Selhorst. Fr. Selhorst wrote on the 16th that Fr. Kilian was "on his way home. He may get there before this letter reaches you (Father Provincial)." [5]

Fr. Kilian had served his country and his companions in the 92nd commendably for nearly three years. Having seen them through the worst, he was now free to make a quick exit home. Whatever fate awaited him next did not really matter. He was after all, a soldier, and like all soldiers he longed more than ever to visit his family and friends. Fr. Kilian never regretted his decision to join the army. His sentiments were identical to that of his friend Fr. Selhorst, who would write, "The twenty months I have spent overseas are worth twenty years of experience." [6]

Most of the members of the 92nd would eventually reach home by

Christmas of 1945. For the vast majority of them, they would not see each other again until Fr. Kilian organized their first reunion in Wakeeney, Kansas, some 30 years later. By then, most of Fr. Kilian's "boys" would be grandfathers, and most of the officers would be senior citizens.

Fr. Kilian wrote another story about the long voyage home. He describes in detail the events and emotions surrounding soldiers who are on their way home for the first time in years. It is also a reminder that war changes men, and that for many ex-soldiers, the war will always be with them.

"The Lost Battalion"

By every measure of intelligence, gratitude and goodwill, joyous occasions should never be turned into dour experiences or depressing overcasts. And yet, that is precisely what happened in Manila Bay as we boarded the troop ship anxiously waiting to take us stateside in September of 1945. Yes, the war was over- barely. But the stark reality of that fact had not yet registered in full. We still looked at every soldier with suspicion. Is he really a friend or foe? Even after passing thousands of fellow American soldiers, the apprehension subconsciously persisted. It was a terrible feeling, even a treasonous feeling. Only time could eradicate that demon. And that too came to pass.

To start the voyage home RIGHT, I decided to have Mass and a general service on deck, immediately upon boarding, namely before the sun bade farewell to heaven and earth and all on or in the Southwest Pacific. I had hardly begun to set up my altar, when a tightly-knit group approached me and said, "Father, may we set up your altar or prepare for the general service, all the way across the sea? We will find, on a daily basis, the best place, prepare the basic materials, and secure the best time. To this we have committed ourselves long ago."

Be assured it was at this point, that my apprehension totally dissolved. Naturally, I became justifiably anxious, if not curious about this group. Time again played its part, and without fail. In days to come I came to know the ghastly story in all its gory dimensions.

They were in all, seven; two First Lieutenants and five enlisted men, Catholic and Protestants, respectively. As I soon learned in deepest and greatest detail, they were the remnant, the sole survivors of an entire reconnaissance battalion. (A battalion might have as many as seven to eight hundred men). They secretly stole into New Guinea long before we actually invaded the island. It was their mission, literally, to scour the huge jungle island to ascertain where the enemy was mostly concentrated, where the greatest danger existed, where and how food could best be scrounged, and where an army of that size could best be hidden.

Not surprisingly, their kindest allies turned out to be missionaries and their flocks — all staunch and loyal American friends.

But as they soon experienced, even with the kind help of their newly-made friends, the unpredictable task took its dire toll. There were: malaria, jungle rot, scrub typhus, beriberi and malnutrition to mention just a few hazards. One, or all, made their deadly attack on the heroic troops. One by one, they quickly succumbed to the hungry jaws of the vast jungle. Yes, even the stalwart commanding officers fell one by one, day by day.

When and before, the last officer died he would commission in the field the most qualified enlisted soldier who automatically took over command. Military headquarters would automatically acknowledge and confirm the commission when notified.

The two Lieutenants, so commissioned, were Lt. Bourdeau and Lt. Breveaux. In their group were five enlisted men of various ranks. After weeks of intense living and fighting, and after seeing hundreds of their men die for whatever cause, they solidified into one strong, powerful unit. Both lieutenants were Catholics and the enlisted men were both Catholic and non-Catholic, respectively. All had by now, one tremendous resolve — no one would die without the best medical help possible, even at great risk, much less without spiritual help. The boast of both lieutenants was that none of their comrades died without the comfort of a loving Heavenly Father at their side. It was also their consolation and reward.

Before we rescued them, after the invasion, they took a solemn oath that for the rest of their lives they would attend services according to each man's convictions. I need hardly belabor the thought that they lived that oath to the hilt, all the way across the ocean.

However, it was only a matter of time when Lt. Bourdeau became overwhelmingly haunted with his past terrible experiences. He would torment me by the hours and hours — day and night. No argument could assuage his fears, regrets, doubts, anxieties or his imaginary guilt. Over an over, and ten hundred times over, he would <u>even openly</u> rebel against God — that he did not die with his comrades on the island. Because <u>they</u> were dead and <u>he</u> was still alive, he felt like a traitor to his men. Many more times than before he would remind me that if he had died with his unit he would now, like them, be in heaven and from there pray for the remnant and his country. Naturally, I conjured up all the arguments hidden in my brain to calm his fears and anxieties but to no avail.

But at long last came an old German proverb to my support. It is: "Enlich is nicht eveg." What comes to an end is not eternal.

After fully a month on the sea, we finally neared the Golden Gate. A soldier no more than ten feet from me, looking through his binoculars, spied the Golden Gate first. Instantly, he threw his binoculars into the air, shouted with all his strength and with total abandon, "The Golden Gate!!" Thousands of necks craned, the better to see the Golden Gate, but it was not yet visible to the naked eye.

But shortly, yes, after nearly three years of anticipation, the Golden Gate itself did come within sight of even the naked eye. An ear-splitting howl went up, all the way to the heavens and back. Soldiers, officers and crew members rudely forced their way — the better to see — until the ship began to list. Objects of all sorts were thrown into the air or into the ocean itself, never to be recovered nor ever to be sought. The Golden Gate was all that mattered. It declared loudly and clearly and definitively, "We are home, we are safe at last, we are among friends, families, sweethearts, wives and parents."

I stood silently and stoically by the rail as I had done hundreds of times, totally mesmerized with the deep, deep conflicting emotions. It was at this intensely critical moment that two fiercely strong arms encircled the upper part of my body — ready to crush every bone. A head rested on my shoulder and through all the hysteria and commotion and shouting, tears fell copiously on my shoulder. A voice ever so softly, ever so sincerely whispered into my ear, "Father, now that I have seen the Golden Gate, I am no longer angry with God — that I did not die in the jungle. Now I want to live and make this our country a better place for us all, and to thank God and my lost battalion for the price they paid, that I might live to fulfill my service to God and country — my self-assigned task."

At Stoneman I saw him daily, even hourly. He never lost his resolve. For many, many years later I heard from him. He had married, raised a beautiful family and worked indefatigably to make this our country a better place. But "enlich is nicht evig." Even him I finally lost because he was not "evig." But never, no never, have I forgotten the traumatic experience.

Chapter 16

Home Sweet Home

In later years, Fr. Kilian would increasingly come to appreciate the time that he spent with the 92nd Evacuation Hospital. Their shared experiences had created extremely strong bonds of friendship and respect. He considered this a great blessing, especially as he grew older and he noticed that other retired priests were growing lonelier as their families gradually passed away. Fr. Kilian's family by contrast was growing as he aged. He would later come to know and love the children of his army companions, and their grandchildren, for we were all part of the family of the 92nd. By the grace of God, we would come to know and love him as well.

After the Second World War, Fr. Kilian would spend two more years in the service of his country. First however, he needed to see his home. Home for Fr. Kilian meant Kansas, where the laughter of his brothers, sisters and dear mother mingled with the familiar sights, smells and tastes of the large Dreiling family gatherings. Theirs was a family that lived life fully and completely. Any gathering was cause for celebration, so we can only imagine the joy and love that must have been shared upon the safe return of not one, but two of their brave sons from such a costly war. While Fr. Kilian had served in the Pacific, his brother Paul had survived very tall odds as a gunner of a B-17 crew serving in Europe. Paul would later suffer greatly as a result of the guilt he felt at being the only surviving member of his flight crew.

In the same story that Fr. Kilian would later dedicate to "mothers all over the world," he relates to us some of the details of this first visit home after the war.

"From the time I enlisted in early July of 1943 until I was ordered to do duty in the land of occupation in 1946, mother matured, grew stronger, certainly far more reconciled to accept the world and even people in it as they are, and not as she wished they were.

"Thus, when I came home on leave before going to Europe, I brought three sergeants with me. She thoroughly enjoyed the young men. She cooked incessantly and bent to their every desire. They in turn, reciprocated cheerfully. It was a fun-packed three weeks. The kind you can only feel, never adequately explain. All the neighbors envied our house. With every volley of laughter that erupted from our house their desire to join us increased.

"But once more, the inevitable time to face reality loomed high above the horizon. I had to say 'good bye.' To ease the tension, I side-tracked the real issue by imploring her to be more outgoing. To all of this she gave me an attentive ear. In fact, a sympathetic ear. But her only reply remains 'a statement of the nation' for all times. She said, 'child, God gave to all of us a miraculous memory. It is the storehouse from which old age draws its food for thought. You are young, vigorous, vibrant and much inexperienced. You need to see, to touch, to hear, to taste and love all good things. It is your harvest time, your gathering into your storehouse. I have done my homework long ago. My storehouse is full, pressed down and flowing over. All I need to do is to dip into it, bring out the very best and thankfully, enjoy its fruits. Indeed, I often neglect my work because I am too preoccupied with arranging and rearranging my priorities. And recall child, that you have only the present to draw from. I have a past of 72 years, plus the present, plus the future, which the wise say is the sum total of the past and the present in one. So child, banish all concern. Your mother is far too busy in her occupational armchair thinking to be lonesome.'

"I surrendered. I had no more comments. In spite of my formidable education and my maturing experience during the war, I was no match for my mother. Once more I conceded, 'Old age must be wisdom on the march.' "

Fr. Kilian astutely observed that the war changed not only the combatants, but also those on the home front as well. His own mother had become somehow stronger and wiser as a result of her own experiences.

It has been said that behind every great man is a great woman. In Agnes Dreiling, Fr. Kilian had an excellent role model. Her living example of loving and caring for others, along with her simple wisdom and love of life were traits that Fr. Kilian valued and possessed in great measure.

Fr. Kilian's first visit home after the war passed all too quickly. He describes, "From the time I parted my unit until I walked into my mother's house, time dragged at a snail's pace. Hours turned into days and days into months. But once I entered my mother's house the reverse was true. Days turned into hours and months into days. In other words, Father Time reversed gears." [1]

There was another "home" that Fr. Kilian longed to see as well. St. Charles Seminary saw many beautiful reunions in late 1945 and early 1946. At one time, there were 47 priests from the C.PP.S. in the armed services during WWII, including Fr. John Wilson, who had survived three years of imprisonment at the hands of the Japanese. One from their ranks, Fr. Klement Falter, had given his life early in the war during the invasion of Morocco. [2]

The Second World War brought about great changes within the C.PP.S. In the words of Father Provincial Joseph Marling, "It is no exaggeration to say that no other labors in which we are engaged have so attracted the attention and concern of all the Fathers, as has the work of our Chaplains in the army and navy." [3] After the war, the society would search for another cause worthy of the energy and passion demonstrated by her sons during the war. They would soon turn their attention Southward to Latin America. At the call of Pope Pius XII to help preserve the Catholic faith in South America, the C.PP.S. sent many missionaries to Chile. Many of the parishes there were abandoned and had no priests available.

With a nucleus of young, energetic priests who had been tested by the fires of war, the C.PP.S. did not have a problem finding volunteers for this South American adventure. Many of the priests sent to Chile were former army or navy chaplains. This new mission was to be headed up by none other than Fr. John Wilson himself. [4] To this day there are C.PP.S. priests working in South America, planting and cultivating the seeds of faith, including Fr. Kilian's nephew, Gaylord

Dreiling. Gaylord is one of the many who were inspired by Kilian's stories and by his example. He has labored as a pastor in the city of Lima, Peru for over 30 years.

Fr. Kilian's life would follow a different path. After the war, Fr. Kilian decided to re-enlist for another two years. After witnessing so many brave young men offer up their lives for their country, Fr. Kilian still wanted to do more. When he re-enlisted, he was under the impression that he would be assigned to the occupying army in Japan. However, Uncle Sam had other plans.

Fr. Kilian's first assignment would be to the army of occupation in Europe, and it would begin another great adventure for him. His fluency in the German language made him very valuable to the American Army, and he did not go unnoticed by the military intelligence office. During this assignment, he would travel to most of the free European countries and meet many famous and fascinating people. He would also add to his reputation as a dynamic and skilled leader and a humanitarian.

For four months however, he remained in the U.S. During the Christmas season of 1945, he was temporarily assigned to Fletcher Center Hospital in Cambridge, Ohio. [5] His genuine concern, compassion and even reverence for the young men physically and emotionally scarred from the fighting, including the German POW's, is apparent in this next story.

"X-mas of 1945 at Snuffy's"

Before I was completely "recycled," I was once more standing at the rail of a troop ship (as I had done hundreds of times in the Pacific), going not to Japan but Europe. Looking over the vast waters, contemplating its power and beauty as well as its potential danger, I had ample time to reach into my storehouse and bring out, for sheer personal enjoyment, the good things of the past 4 months. One choice morsel was X-mas of 1945 at Fletcher Center Hospital in Cambridge, OH. For example, I had 2700 patients, 7-1/2 miles of hallways, 3 wards of men who had been in the Bataan Death March, and a fine officer as CO of the hospital who faithfully, though not a Catholic, attended mass from his office over the intercom every

Sunday. We nicknamed him "Snuffy." With this blessed package, also came a wonderful group of Red Cross gals and German prisoners, all prophetic helpers.

Because X-mas was fast approaching, I had to act fast! Elsie Eagles, head of the Red Cross group, and a fine Christian, quickly surfaced as my organist. More, she took over the formidable task of decorating and arranging the chapel for X-mas Midnight Mass. High above the altar for example, she inserted crèche; namely figurines that I quickly snatched and brought out of the prison camp of Cabanatuan on Luzon, P.I. when we released the prisoners. (It, the crib, became eventually a national concern and attraction). But more importantly, she made ready the chapel for the Midnight Mass. With the aid of the chief nurse, she commandeered enough nurses to bring all bedfast patients into the chapel on "stretchers-on-wheels." These she arranged solidly around the altar until it looked like a huge sunflower. In the center aisle she ran two rows of stretchers all the way back. At the back she turned right and left. The side aisles were left free. From the choir loft the design looked exactly like a huge chalice, with cup, stem and base. One might say a chalice make of broken human bodies and some broken souls. Indeed, a most impressive sight. In the windows she placed red vigil lights. While the lights in the main were still turned off the vigil lights played and flickered, to bring the sheets and the faces of the patients mysteriously alive. It too was a grand sight. The rest of the chapel was packed with ambulatory patients. The mass was sung by the German prisoners in typical Wagnerian virility. However, the important X-mas music was played by our hostess, Miss Elsie Eagles. After the sermon and Mass, in which I strongly appealed for peace throughout the world, Elsie intoned "Let There Be Peace." It was sung softly, oh ever so softly, but just as intensely and emotionally. The final flare came when Elsie struck the mighty "Battle Hymn of the Republic." She gave full and free sway to the organ by releasing every stop. The patients and congregation took to the battle field and instantly sang with absolute abandon. Broken bodies rose ever so slightly on elbows to simulate participation. Some could do no more than raise their eyes to heaven; others kept time with their remaining one arm or their remaining one leg. The sight was heart-breaking. Yes, it was a sad, sad demonstration, but also a grand sight because it so dramatically expressed what is so strongly American: loyalty, truth, courage, patriotism and above all faith.

At the end I thanked them profusely and no one doubted my sincerity because every word was thoroughly cleansed with tears; theirs and mine. Also, it made for a cheerful X-mas long after, still referred to as "X-mas of 1945 at Snuffys."

Chapter 17

Return to the Ancestral Homeland

Fr. Kilian was at first, disappointed at not being able to stay in the U.S. However, he never seemed to feel sorry for himself for very long. His life had become a recurring pattern of making the very best of each and every situation in which God had placed him. By now a veteran of long sea voyages, Fr. Kilian enjoyed striking up conversations in order to meet new people and to pass the time. During the voyage to Europe, he had an uplifting experience upon meeting a former U.S. army pilot who was also travelling to Germany.

"One Returned to Give Thanks"

The great and costly war, WWII, was over. However, here I was holding desperately to the rail of the ship, fighting angrily the mighty waves of the Atlantic. Everything to date was simply old shoe — repetition. I had had all that and infinitely more during the war in the Pacific. But what was I now, doing here on a ship headed for the Army of Occupation? Recall, after my first return from the Pacific after VJ Day, I vowed never to desert American soil, rather dedicate myself to promoting genuine and sincere loyalty to this country and the principles for which so many, many died in the Pacific and Europe. For that very solemn reason alone, I agreed to sign up for still another hitch in the army with the understanding that I would never again see foreign land, least of all in time of war, or so-called war. Perhaps the best and most honest answer to my own questions was that one did not learn the Army in depth, fighting in foxholes, jungles, swamps or high seas. These experiences were, one might say, experiences over and above the linc of ordinary duty, so I thought. I soon learned differently.

I had hardly signed up for another stretch in the peacetime army, when orders came 'loud and clear.' "Report to Kilmer for duty in the Army of Occupation." I accepted the order neither gracefully, much less calmly. In fact, I rebelled vocally and above all, mentally, but to no avail. However, even rebellion can have its reward. By the time I finally returned stateside in late 1947, my rewards were, indeed, many, very many, and the price equally great in terms of malaria, amoebic dysentery and general anemia. Some, like the after effects of malaria, would stay with me for nearly 45 years. This dubious reward, among others, nevertheless remains a tremendously rich experience.

One incident I experienced even before we had left N.Y. by day, was a mellowing encounter with a most interesting officer standing, as I often did, by the rail and looking out into the unknown — thinking, thinking, and thinking still harder and longer. Unknowingly, I espoused his cause almost miraculously, as I was soon to learn.

The officer, who was once a pilot, was shot down over Germany, bailed out and landed, of all places, in the farmyard of an elderly couple. In landing, he broke his one leg and injured more members of his body and soul than he ever suspected he had. Nature and a merciful hand above relieved him — he promptly faded into blissful unconsciousness. When again he surfaced, he found himself not in a prison camp, but in the darkest and the deepest bowels of the earth — a sub-cellar under their farmhouse. The kindly couple rescued him, hid him, splintered his fractured leg as best they could; profusely poured the proverbial oil into his wounds, but above all, cleverly went about their business, doing their chores as though nothing had happened. Naturally, with the least and primitive medical care, he suffered greatly and for quite some time. A doctor was nearby, but he was a staunch S.S. officer and could never be trusted. And so he lived in this subterranean apartment much like a prairie dog, for two and a half years. To pass the time he taught the elderly couple English and they taught him German. Both eventually became proficient in each other's tongues. They, the elderly couple, became the silver lining in a raging hurricane above and ahead. True, the recovery was far from perfect. The bones did not knit well, nor perfectly, but his soul recovered with miraculous additions of well-being. I need hardly belabor the fact that he developed into a mild, gentle, truly grateful and very, very lovable human being, or as a kind friend said of me one time, "He is a man worth loving." Yes, he was recaptured, this time by the U.S. Army.

Only after a lengthy discussion did he turn to me and say, "And now chaplain, you must wonder what I am doing returning to Germany after all that horrible experience. Well, I am the one returning to give thanks. You see, I have in my pocket, enough money to keep that couple for many, many years and more. Our government generously provided for them and it is all in my pocket to give wholeheartedly and gratefully. You see chaplain, war is not all hell. It leaves room for goodness, kindness and gratitude, and I carry all these happily with me to be laid at the feet of my protectors, and with absolute and complete gratitude."

Late, very late, we parted as the stars twinkled brightly overhead. I watched him hobble to the gangway with a blessed inner joy; indeed, a strange inner joy that I now felt, justified my returning to active service even in a foreign land, and fortunately, a land not at war. The reward: meeting my friend and his beautiful experience, plus a whole world full of experiences that I never would have had, except for my tour of duty in the Army of Occupation. At Bremmerhaven we parted, he to his mission of mercy, and I to Heidelberg and eventually to nearly every part of Europe where there was military, and where new and exciting experiences awaited my every turn in the road — experiences that I stored safely in my secret closet, my memory, and from which I draw daily, copiously, to entertain or inform audiences and, indeed, myself, for is not the memory the storehouse into which old age dips and brings out the best for body and soul? And to the very last hour of life?

It is interesting to note that when Fr Kilian recorded this story in January of 1992, he used his mother's own analogy of "drawing from a secret storehouse" of memories, to "entertain or inform" others and himself. Fr. Kilian wrote this story when he was 86 years old and living in "retirement" at the seminary at Carthagena, OH. We are indeed fortunate that he lived long enough to leave us a written record of this and other events.

Fr. Kilian reminds us again that from every evil, inevitably, there emerges something good. Fr. Kilian's God is a merciful, forgiving God. His message to us therefore, is also one of reconciliation. He clearly understood the healing power of forgiveness, and he profoundly wanted us to understand it as well. He reminds us that within Germany there were many good people of faith who felt powerless to stop the Nazi war machine. They too lost sons and daughters in the great conflict of WWII.

The older couple in this last story saw an opportunity to voice their opinion when an American pilot parachuted into their back yard. To appreciate this act of kindness, mercy and courage, we should remember that to harbor the enemy in Germany during a time of war was considered "treason," and was punishable by death. Many American airmen were not as fortunate as the pilot who met Fr. Kilian. Quite a few were welcomed to Germany at the end of a farmer's pitchfork, and never lived to see a prison camp. From the perspective of the German people, they were dropping bombs on the "Fatherland" resulting in the deaths of hundreds of thousands of German civilians.

In the previous story, Fr. Kilian also alludes to some of the illnesses that began to afflict him during this post-war period. Some, like Amoebic dysentery and malaria, were relapses of diseases that he had contracted during the pacific campaign. Fr. Kilian would suffer from these as well as others off and on, for the rest of his life. His struggles with illness would also shape his character. In time, he would learn to accept these bouts of illness as learning and growth experiences, and would take advantage of the idle time provided to pray, reflect and commit his most cherished memories to paper. However, in the early post-war years, his recurring bouts of ill health were little more than annoyances or impediments to the achievement of his objectives. They did however have the effect of forcing him to slow down from his usual, frenetic pace.

It was while Fr. Kilian was stationed in Frankfort that he was sent on the "secret mission" described in the first chapter "Confession of the Beast." This was just one of the many significant events that occurred during Fr. Kilian's tour of duty in Europe.

As Fr. Kilian states in the previous story, he considered his time with the U.S. Army of occupation to be a great adventure, full of new and exciting challenges. As always, he would work steadfastly to improve the lot of U.S. soldiers as well as that of the local civilian population. Fr. Kilian's fluency in the German language, actually his first language, would have afforded him opportunities to learn a great deal more about the German people than his peers ever could have. He would again demonstrate his considerable charm and where necessary, his political skills and growing connections. He would meet many fascinating people. Some, like the Prince Archbishop of Austria were also powerful and influential.

Fr. Kilian describes in this next story, how he was able to utilize his relationship with the Prince Archbishop to cut through bureaucratic red tape, when the sale of the Von Trapp family estate to the C.PP.S. Brothers became "complicated" by speculators.

"All Is Calm...All Is Bright"

As chaplain in the Army of Occupation in the European Theater in 1946 and 1947, I gave two or three missions in Salzburg, Austria to our scattered military personnel. While there, I repeatedly met, and fortunately therefore came to know, Prince Archbishop of Salzburg. He was a man of extraordinary power and authority. Because of that I cleverly, perhaps insidiously is the better term, but innocently manipulated the good Archbishop.

Bishop Joseph Marling, C.PP.S, our superior at that time, had written to me previously to my coming to Salzburg and pleaded that I intervene - bring to a prompt solution the transaction of the Von Trapp Family Estate. It was to be the American gift to our C.PP.S. Community in Austria — shortly after VJ Day. (For the time being, they were living in a garret with little or no heat, and running water only on the first floor. I visited them every so often and each time came away deathly cold and hungry.)

When the decisive letter of appeal arrived from the states, I immediately took it to whom? Naturally, to Prince Archbishop! He read it carefully and laid it on his desk. As his fist came down hard he said, "Father we will resolve this problem 'augenblicklich' — at once." With that he reached for the phone, spoke to the party on the other end in beautiful German but in no uncertain terms, "Contact lawyer 'John Doe', and conclude that Von Trapp Family Estate 'augenblicklich' instantly." Within a few weeks the Precious Blood Fathers in Austria were handed the deed of the estate. The crisis was thus resolved, thanks to Prince Archbishop. (The lawyer had hoped that the transaction would collapse and he then would be in a position to initiate a better deal for himself.)

Before leaving Salzburg for still another mission, I went to see the Archbishop to thank him for his expertise in bringing the transaction to an unexpected but swift resolution. The Archbishop regretted my leaving the area and in expressing his gratitude he said, "But Father, you are not leaving Salzburg without going to Oberndorf. Nobody comes to Salzburg without visiting Oberndorf." I said, "But what is in Oberndorf that I should see?" He replied, "The grave of Father Joseph Mohr, who wrote the beautiful and endearing song, "Stille Nacht, Heilige Nacht."

Time was of the essence. I had to move fast — 'schnell, scharf, blitzlich.' Within hours I commandeered about a dozen people: chaplains and interested military personnel. Also, we commandeered a huge army vehicle and that very night, with a trustworthy guide, we drove to Oberndorf, some 25 miles west of Salzburg. On the way to Oberndorf I taught them the first stanza of Stille Nacht.

It was a bitter, bitter cold night, but the entire sky was a heavenly, a brilliantly transparent blue. The stars dangled precariously by the millions from the azure blue and in breathtaking brightness and quiet. To us it seemed that each star vied with its neighbor, indeed, to outshine its neighbor — the better to show us the quickest and best way to the grave of Fr. Mohr. As we disembarked at the cemetery gate, we slowly, ever so slowly, ever so silently and ever so reverently proceeded to Fr. Mohr's grave. Softly, I intoned Stille Nacht 'sub voce!' But as we came closer and closer to the grave, our pitch rose higher and higher, louder and louder. At the actual sight of the memorial grave stone, all irresistibly and reverently knelt around the grave in absolute, holy silence. Naturally, we said a prayer of grateful thanksgiving to Fr. Mohr for his near miraculous legacy to all the world, but again, all in sacred and abated silence.

The stars too joined our forces by fiercely playing on our imagination and physical well being.

When nearly frozen to the marrow of our bones, we reluctantly rose and returned to our transportation. As we did, I once more intoned, ever so softly, Silent Night, but this time in English. Cold but happy, we gave our utmost best as we sang the unforgettable, the lovable song Silent Night. Yes, we did it with reckless abandon but with a grateful heart.

No, we had no candles as they did in the Congregational Church in Redding, CT, but we had something infinitely greater and better; we had the overpoweringly dazzling lights of a million STARS and the awesome quiet of the night, — all to lead and guide us eventually to a still greater traditional LIGHT, — the Holy Infant. With boast, we agreed that we had not only one lone Brilliant Star as at Bethlehem, we had millions of Stars — all at our disposal just for remembering and loving the Holy Infant even more intensely than Fr. Mohr.

For nearly fifty years now, I have recalled and related this remarkable event at Christmas time, but never with less than angelic joy and love and good, intense feeling toward <u>all men</u>. The joy, namely that the choir of Angels expressed so universally when they sang, "Glory to God in the highest and Peace to men of goodwill."

While reading Fr. Kilian's story "All is Calm...All is Bright," one can almost feel the nip of the cold night air. Fr. Kilian paints a vivid picture for us through his careful word selection and by his recollection of small details. One gets the impression that to spend time with Kilian was to experience life more fully, more completely. Not only did Fr. Kilian seize upon the wondrous opportunities that life presented him, he clearly appreciated the "little things," so often overlooked that bring us joy. Fr. Kilian appreciated the value of spontaneity. His openness to impromptu opportunities and his willingness to approach total strangers afforded him some of his most interesting experiences and widened his circle of friends.

One of Fr. Kilian's best friends from this period was Colonel Al

Burnett. Burnett was a gifted army officer who had been promoted to full Colonel by age 27. Like many others, he was attracted by Fr. Kilian's charm, wisdom and warmth, and generally enjoyed his company. A strong, mutual bond of friendship and respect developed between Fr. Kilian and Col. Burnett. They also found time to have some fun. Many years later, Col. Burnett offered a few recollections of his two years with Fr. Kilian in post-WWII Europe.

"I will never forget the good Padre. He's kind of like a broken leg, hard to forget. The Catholic hierarchy made a wise choice when they gave him this assignment...The Padre very nearly recruited me. If our assigned orders hadn't separated us when they did, I'd probably be a loyal member of his flock today. Whether or not I'd be richer in my soul I leave it to the theologian to argue. One thing for sure, with his talent of separating the guys from the women, I'd be a lot poorer in the line (a reference to Kilian's success in recruiting candidates for the priesthood). I became acquainted with the Padre shortly after we both found ourselves stationed in Germany in 1946.

"The Padre, who was stationed in Frankfort, wanted to fly to Heidelburg, so he got himself assigned down there. I was in Heidelburg too. I figured anybody with his contacts was worth knowing, so I started attending his chapel services (Burnett was not a Catholic). Pretty soon, you would have thought I had been a Catholic all my life. I knew when they rang the bells and all about the incense. One time I asked him about the practice of confession and he very patiently explained the doctrine to me. He never got me in the mood though. A character like him might have used it against me." [1]

On one occasion, Fr. Kilian invited Burnett to accompany him on a trip to Rome. Burnett had just returned from the U.S., where he had been shocked to find that his fiancée was engaged to another man! Fr. Kilian suggested the trip to his young friend in order to help take his mind off the situation back home.

Burnett continues, "Seems like the Padre had a real taste for the wine and that's one thing the Italians had plenty of. So every time the train stopped, he'd swap some of our cigarettes for a bottle of Chianti. It's a good thing the Pope didn't see him when he got to Rome or the Padre might have been out looking for a new job!

"The Padre was a big help. None of us spoke Italian, but they still celebrated Mass in Latin in those days. The Padre seemed always to be gambling in church with dominoes. Anyway, his Latin was very helpful and we never lacked for Chianti. He said Mass in St. Peter's. That probably cost him a few more Chesterfields or Lucky Strikes or a bottle of wine." [1]

By almost all accounts, Fr. Kilian was the best kind of friend. Understanding, concerned and compassionate, he was also fun loving. When Col. Burnett returned to Germany after being rebuffed by his fiancée, Fr. Kilian knew just what he needed. When Burnett swore that he would "stay a bachelor for the next 5,000 years," Fr. Kilian was quick to offer some fatherly advice.

"Face it son, when you are 75 years old and you're sitting on your swing and swinging to and fro, and the women pass by, with each woman that passes you will say, 'Should I have married her?' " [1]

Col. Burnett did learn to love again, and his wife Antonette would join Fr. Kilian's ever-growing circle of friends. Fr. Kilian would also have high praise for Col. Burnett. Of Burnett he would say, "I mean he was a terrific man. He was concerned about everybody under his command. He was such a wonderful guy, and I would like to think that I had a little something to do with that." [1]

This last statement indicates that Fr. Kilian was well aware of the positive impact that he had upon the lives of those around him. One senses that within Fr. Kilian there was a glimmer of pride in his own accomplishments, especially in his ability to bring out the best in those around him. For all of Fr. Kilian's remarkable talents and abilities, he was quick to admit that he was not perfect. He has been described as a "complex" man with a larger than average ego. If one were to look for weaknesses within Fr. Kilian's makeup, it could be said of him that perhaps he enjoyed hearing the many compliments and the steep praise that he received a little too much. Fr. Kilian was certainly comfortable with the limelight, if he didn't actually enjoy it. Some thought that he did enjoy it.

However, Fr. Kilian was not a boastful man. He would never bore the uninterested observer with his stories. In fact, many priests who knew Fr. Kilian in later years remarked that he told them very little of his wartime experiences. He purposely avoided the subject of the war around other former army chaplains because he knew how painful it was to open up old wounds. Better than most, he knew that any chaplain who had seen combat likely carried emotional, if not physical scars around with them for the rest of their lives.

Fr. Kilian had an excellent ability to read people, and he knew when someone was genuinely interested and listening. (He could also recognize when someone was hurting). If he told one of his stories from the pulpit, it was to drive home some very relevant point. For an attentive and appreciative audience, his eyes would light up and he would become more animated. His voice would rise and fall, quicken or slow down for emphasis, as if perfected over the years. While his written stories paint vivid pictures for us, hearing Fr. Kilian tell them in person was riveting.

His world was bigger than that of most of his contemporaries because of all that he had seen and done, and he accepted as his mission the task of enlightening others through what he had learned. Even if he did enjoy receiving the compliments of others, they were nonetheless deserved. And who among us does not enjoy a kind word or recognition for our own accomplishments. Are they not the fruits of our labor? For Fr. Kilian, kind words were the only recognition that he received for his lifetime of labor in the service of his Lord Jesus. Once, I asked him why he did not allow someone to compile his life's beautiful stories into a book. His response was, "No, perhaps after I'm gone someone will want do that, but that is for someone else."

In truth, Fr. Kilian was a confident man who was aware of his many talents. Yet, his experiences taught him the beauty and the value of humility. He loved the poor, the downtrodden and the dispossessed, as he worked feverishly to improve their plight. He lived very simply and perhaps due to his impoverished childhood, felt a strong connection to the poor.

While stationed in Vienna, Fr. Kilian had another rather harrowing experience. At the time, a portion of Vienna was still occupied by Soviet troops. While being driven to his hotel, Fr. Kilian's military driver unwittingly made a wrong turn and plunged into the Soviet section of the city. His escort was worried about the fate of Fr. Kilian should he fall into Soviet hands, due to his Russian/German heritage. Rather than explaining to the Soviet guards that a mistake had occurred, the driver decided to streak through the Soviet barricade on the assumption that the Russians wouldn't dare take the initiative and shoot. Fortunately, the driver was right.

Fr. Kilian would laugh as he told this story in later years saying, "The American soldier knows what to do. The Russians didn't have a chance to get orders from headquarters." [2] Fr. Kilian believed that one of the strengths of the American soldier was his ability to improvise and think for himself.

Fr. Kilian recorded one more story from his years with the army of occupation in Europe. He wrote this story in the last years of his life, when his health was failing him. We must infer from this that it was an important event for him because it was only with extreme effort that he was able to type the article himself.

"The Best Kept Secret at the Camp of Infamy"

A silver lining of divine hope hovered over Dachau, the camp of infamy, during its darkest and most dangerous days. This is the story of how one man brought a taste of heaven to those who were experiencing hell on earth.

As post chaplain of Heidelberg, Germany, one of my official duties was to participate in all parades at a moment's notice. The occasion could be a civic celebration or the honoring of an official dignitary. One day in September, 1947, there was a parade to honor a French General named Gray, who at one time carried on a tremendously successful underground warfare against both Hitler and Mussolini. However, when an informer had brought about his downfall, he spent four and a half years in the German concentration camp at Dachau.

I stood next to him on the reviewing stand as battalions passed by in review. He had on a brand new American uniform and wore it with daring and pride. Though only forty seven, he appeared near ninety. Though he tried to stand at perfect attention, his emaciated body kept sagging back into a most embarrassing posture. I watched out of the corner of my eye and felt sorry for him. At one point during the parade, he nudged me gently and asked, "Chaplain, are you a Catholic priest?" I assured him that I was. In broken English he added, "Could I see you after the parade?"

After the parade he took me by the arm and led me off some twenty or thirty feet. Waving his oversized arms, he said, "Father, this parade is a great honor, but I have had a far greater honor in Dachau. The Holy Father, Pius XII, permitted me to carry on my person the Holy Eucharist. And even more, he permitted me to distribute the Holy Communion to bishops, priests, and Catholic lay people. To indicate where I would distribute that night, I would sit in a certain spot for nearly an hour during the afternoon. All would know that there is where I would give out Holy Communion. For nearly four years we carried on this deceptive practice right under the noses of the guards, and they never suspected or discovered us."

I asked him why he was chosen rather than the bishops or priests to give Communion.

"Father, they searched the bishops and priests daily. They never suspected a rogue like me. Besides that, I was insolent to both priests and bishops in presence of the guards. Sometimes I even did them physical harm. They suffered it gladly to keep up the façade."

"But General, where did you get the consecrated hosts?"

"That," he said, "was the best kept secret of Dachau. Seven of Hitler's most trusted SS guards took turns going to Catholic churches where the pastors would give them the hosts to sneak back into camp to give to me."

I listened in total amazement. I asked him if that wasn't very dangerous.

"For four years, I and all involved could have been discovered at any time. And we each knew full well if they found out what we were doing, we would be shot or sent to the gas chamber or tortured or even thrown to the starving dogs they kept to tear us apart. We lived with that terror and witnessed it every day."

I never saw General Gray again after that, but I will never forget the joy and delight in his eyes as he told me the story of outsmarting Hitler and carrying Christ to those noble ones who were starving for a taste of hope.

Chapter 18

Facing the Families

The end of Fr. Kilian's service with the U.S. Army was also the end of the most defining period of his life. He would never again view the world in quite the same way.

He would live for another 50 years, almost another lifetime. He would labor in the service of his Lord Jesus and the C.PP.S. as much as his health would allow, for nearly all of those 50 years. He would face debilitating illnesses on quite a few occasions, but just when his friends thought he was finished, he would somehow "miraculously" recover and resume new priestly duties.

Upon his return, one of the most difficult tasks Fr. Kilian faced was visiting the families of loved ones who had died in his arms. He had made promises to many, that he would try his best to relay their last words to their mother, father, brother, wife etc... He found the performance of this task daunting and emotionally draining. Nevertheless, he charged forward and visited as many family members as he could, because he knew how important it was for them to hear what they longed to hear; a final message from their lost loved one.

On Fr. Kilian's return voyage home to the U.S. in 1947, he met another chaplain on yet another ship's rail. The man, who had seen more than his share of the horrors of war, seemed disturbed. By confiding in Fr. Kilian, he would begin an almost unbelievable sequence of events, resulting in the following powerful story about the power of faith.

"Xmas Wrapped in Brown"

It has been said, and many times over, that only God can bring good out of evil. It has also been said, and many more times, that war is hell.

Now 80 years old, and nearly 52 years in the priesthood, I concur wholeheartedly. Years of intensive book learning planted a hungry desire for even greater knowledge. However, these hard, even cruel, but sometimes beautifully difficult experiences merged it all into one lump of objective reality. It is illustrated in the following rare incident of yesteryears.

Coming stateside, after a stint in Europe in the Army of Occupation, following WWII, II often stood at the rail of the ship and searched the unknown; the invisible, the far beyond, or sometimes simply compared my experiences in the Pacific during the war, with my experiences in the theatre of occupation after the war.

I was not the only one. Frequently, I watched another chaplain standing by the rail, looking out over the ocean and, it seemed, far beyond. I often asked myself — was he merely watching the calm waters, or enjoying the violent waves, or perhaps fearing the angry ocean; or, was he looking beyond all this, as I so often did? I tried to read his thinking, but without success — naturally. But patience paid its weight in gold, and therein lies buried this story.

Inevitably, and eventually, he approached me, quite deliberately and, visibly shaking, said, "Could I talk to you privately?" I assured him that I was a professional master-listener with wartime experiences in the Pacific and occupational duty in Europe. His story was as sincere as it was real.

He, like myself, was on his way back to the states in late 1947. I had been home a few months after VJ Day, before I was shipped to Europe. Now, I was returning to be separated permanently from the service. He was returning for the first time. Why he returned so late, I never ascertained. All I know is that he suffered from a nervous condition. The basic reason, he merely hinted at.

It seemed, so he told me, that after a severely bloody engagement in France, he recklessly rushed into the fray, where even archangels feared to tread. Among the wounded, dying and dead, he most unsuspectingly learned from the dog tags of a dying soldier, that they were both from the same city, Syracuse, NY. I had had the same experience in the Pacific but took it in stride. For him it was more than he could handle. What really unnerved him however, was the fact that the young soldier tried desperately to scribble something on a piece of brown wrapping paper. But before the chaplain could reach him, the pencil had fallen out of his hands, and two fingers left a trail of blood across the fragmented page.

Yes, he was Catholic. Indeed, he wanted to go to confession and before the episode was executed, he had made his confession, was anointed and leaned back totally relaxed and gratefully at peace. But the angel of death lurked nearby. With one last, horrible gasp he said, "Father, I am dying!" The chaplain quickly took him into his arms, and it was there that the soldier died.

It was only after he had concluded the rights for the dying, that the chaplain remembered the piece of brown paper. It was a partially completed letter and, because it is so short, I will quote it verbatim. It read, "Dear Mother... Hail Mary, full of grace..." There was no more. The letter came to a disorderly end.

The chaplain read it over and over and finally wrote on the bottom: "Over." On the opposite side, he wrote his own message and it read: "Dear Madam... Your son ended his life as he ended his letter to you... saying the Hail Mary. I heard his confession, gave him the last rights, and recommended his soul to God. He died in my arms that very instant... Sympathetically yours... Signed a Catholic Chaplain."

The chaplain, even now, strangely remembered no more. Still shaking badly, he now wrestled with still another problem — finding the mother and telling her all. I had also been through this type of experience, in fact over and over, after my return from the Pacific when I called personally upon the families of men who had died on the islands. With this experience, I was able to guide and direct him, but above all, support him. Long after midnight we shook hands and parted.

I never saw much of him after that, in fact never. I greatly feared that the unknown cloud might have overshadowed him again. I prayed that it had not.

At the pier in New York City, we parted once more — he to his assigned destination and I to Carlyle Barracks, PA for my final severance from the army. I never saw or heard from him after that — until...

Many, many years later, I was assigned to a mission circuit in the upstate New York cities of Buffalo, Rochester and Syracuse and their surrounding territories. All three cities as we well know are notorious for snow and cold weather. This was pre-eminently true of Syracuse, where my assignment took me on this particular occasion. Because of the cold and constant snow, I spent most of my time in church reading, writing sermons, hearing confessions, or just praying.

After a few days, I noticed a grand old lady kneeling by the hours in front of our Lady's altar. She prayed unceasingly. One afternoon, when I returned to the rectory for dinner, I innocently asked the pastor who the lady with the great faith in the Mother of Jesus was, and added that I thought she actually spent hours and hours praying. He rose from his chair, visibly excited. He stammered and stuttered, and finally said, "Father, perhaps you should ask her yourself. She will be delighted to tell you her story. However, be prepared. She carries in her prayer book, a letter stained with her son's own blood."

Without further thought or recollection, I did exactly as he suggested. On the next afternoon, immediately after confessions, I gingerly approached her and said, "Grandma, you have a great devotion to our Blessed Lady don't you?"

She looked at me suspiciously and for a long time. Finally, she said, "Father told you didn't he?"

"No Grandma," I replied, "I simply asked him who the lady was with the beautiful devotion to our Lady, and added that I thought you spent hours and hours in prayer."

She still hesitated, but finally said, "Father, you are a young priest. I could well be your mother. I will tell you."

Slowly and methodically, she continued, "I am a widow for many, many years. My son was only months old when his father died. To support my son, and myself I had to work many and long hours. As our son grew older, he resented the fact that I was gone so much and for so long a time. But Father, I had to support us. We were very close, my son and I, but his resentment increased, and there was no way that I could dissolve it. Early in life, he too worked, and we were in no want. But his hate and anger grew with his advancing age. He became bitter and sullen, and one day he vowed that he no longer believed in religion, or prayer, or church. Adamantly, he refused to attend church, and finally he proclaimed boldly that he no longer believed even in God."

"Over and over now, he declared that war was hell, and since war is fought on earth, the earth itself is hell. The ultimate Father? He denied the God who created him. More, he did it with terrible vehemence. It was awful, Father."

"When war broke out, he was drafted. In absolute silence and utter submission, he joined. But, I never heard from him after he left home. Before going overseas however, he came home on furlough. He spent all his time with me. He even went to church with me, but never moved a lip in prayer, that I could detect. It was hard. When the furlough ended, I was almost glad.

"We took a taxi to the railroad station, and in utter, painful silence, we stood side by side, with never a word passing between us. He simply clutched my hand as he used to do as a little boy. As the troop train approached to take him from me, I boldly got on my knees, in the sight of all the people, and softly said, 'Son, there is one promise I would like to extract from you before you leave.' He unsuspectingly said, 'Mother, you know that I will grant you anything you ask.' Daringly and fearfully I said, 'I want you to say three Hail Marys, daily, as long as the war lasts.'

"He grew exceedingly angry, literally threw my hands from his, and replied, 'Mother, you know I no longer believe in religion or prayer or even God.' All this was in the hearing of the huge crowd, but after one, deep breath, he concluded, 'Mother I will say them, not that I believe in prayer, but because I solemnly promised you.'

"With that he turned about face, boarded the train and I never saw him again. Truth is, I never heard from him.

"Two young soldiers came over and lifted me off the floor. One said ever so kindly and sincerely, and with absolute conviction, 'Mother, don't worry about him, he will be all right.' He was so sincere and certain that it frightened me, but I totally believed him. Yes, he literally lifted me out of hell into heaven.

"But Father, I repeat, until the end of the war, I never heard from him. In fact, not even after the war, until this letter came a day before

Christmas, 1945."

With sadness swimming in one eye, and joy in the other, she handed me a piece of brown wrapping paper and said, "Read it Father."

By now I not only recognized the letter but remembered what it said, (Recall I had heard it all at the ship's rail), even the streaks of blood. But I read it dutifully, "Dear Mother... Hail Mary, full of grace..."

There was no more. At the bottom it said, "Over," but I did <u>not</u> turn the letter over. I simply read <u>from memory</u>, "Dear Madam... Your son ended his life as he ended his letter to you...saying the Hail Mary. I heard his confession, gave him the last rites and recommended his soul to God. He died in my arms that very instant... Sympathetically yours... Signed a Catholic Chaplain."

She looked at me in utter disbelief. After she regained her composure she said ever so softly, "And did you <u>also</u> know that I received this letter the day before Christmas, 1945?"

"No Grandma," I said, "but much more importantly, wasn't it a beautiful Christmas present?"

Her reply at last unnerved me, and I wept with her. She said, "Father, the Child Jesus did not bring half as much joy to Mary and Joseph as this letter brought to me Christmas morning, 1945. God can bring good out of evil, and hell is not the earth, is it Father? And my son knows that too now."

"You see Father, my son was lost and now found. He was dead and now is alive."

I immediately hastened to the rectory and sternly confronted the pastor. He instantly began to shake and tremble, and said, "Holy Father in heaven you are white as a sheet. Please come sit down." "Later," I replied, "now, confess, and until you do come clean, you will be burdened for an entire lifetime. What happened, after we parted at the pier in New York City?"

Shamefacedly, he confessed. "First, Father, I never sent the letter. I cracked up. I found the letter some weeks later among my belongings. I sent it home and made sure that she received it — hand-carried — the day before Christmas, 1945. However, on the outside, I wrote, "DO NOT OPEN before Christmas, 1945. That is why she got it and read it for the first time on Christmas, 1945."

"When I returned stateside with you," he continued, "I asked the bishop for assignment to this parish and he kindly consented. But as you say, the thorn is still in my side. Now, perhaps, it will disintegrate. Thank you, Father."

I was not put off that easily. I continued to press ever more forcefully. "Now pray tell, did you recognize me Saturday afternoon when I cam into your rectory?"

"Father," he said, "I swear it, I did not know or recognize you. True, your voice did betray you. As soon as you preached, I kept repeating, 'I heard that voice before. There is only one like it.'"

"But on Thursday night, when you related that most powerful story, I recognized <u>you</u>, along with your <u>voice</u>. You had used the same illustration in your sermon onboard ship, when you conducted Mass that Sunday for all the passengers."

Yes, we talked long into the night, but before retiring I demanded, "Now may I honestly presume that in the near future, you will open up, confess this beautiful episode without being prodded? Remember, when that day comes, you will be totally free of this torment and guilt."

At the end of the mission, I once more lost him, this time for good. But I never lost the part he played in this beautiful story, nor the part Grandma played, nor mine, which was accidental. More importantly, we had positive proof that war is not all hell, that God can and does bring good out of evil, especially when things so good and beautiful happen on Christmas Day!

It is clear from reading "Xmas Wrapped in Brown," that Fr. Kilian considered the act of visiting the families of deceased soldiers a solemn obligation. It gave him the opportunity to fulfill his priestly mission of bringing comfort to those in sorrow. He believed this so passionately that he was intolerant of the behavior of his fellow priest and chaplain, who could not bring himself to confront the departed soldier's grieving mother.

When "coincidences," like those in Fr. Kilain's true story, "Xmas Wrapped in Brown" occur, they force us to examine our own faith.

Are they truly just coincidences, random events where paths must inevitably cross? Alternatively, are the odds against such random occurrences so great that we must acknowledge the possibility that a force is at work here greater than ourselves? One thing is certain. The life of Fr. Kilian Dreiling was full of these types of "coincidences," and many people of faith felt that they had seen or felt the hand of God, working through him.

There were many instances of Fr. Kilian going out of his way to visit surviving family members and to share the stories they so longed to hear. He would provide details about deathbed confessions, last words to family members and sometimes, deathbed conversions. During these meetings, Fr. Kilian's genuine compassion was like a salve placed upon an open wound. The healing effect that these sessions could have upon family members is apparent in this next story. You will recall from Chapter 10 that Fr. Kilian had made a promise to a young soldier as he looked down upon the young man's coffin. He promised to go and visit the young man's "mother, twin sister and family, and tell them all." As you will see from the next story, which is actually the continuation of the story "Johnnie Doe," Fr. Kilian honored this promise.

Johnnie Doe (Cont'd)

In 1948, I was appointed rector of our college seminary. Shortly thereafter an emergency arose. I was ordered to New York City to substitute for a priest who was hospitalized. While there, I found an opening. For three weeks, every afternoon I would go by subway to the Union Station, change, and head for the Athletic Club in lower Manhattan. There I would meet countless families of boys I buried or sent off to eternity. And so it happened that I walked into the spacious sitting room in the club one fine afternoon. A handsome, friendly Irishman met me at once and introduced himself: Phil Mecowen, a son-in-law. He at once pointed out the entire Bow family. But before I met them I said, "Phil, tell me, how much shall I tell them...all?" He promptly replied, "Father, tell them all, they can take it." He introduced me to all the family. After being properly introduced, mother Bow said, "Father, you sit next to me and Daddy you sit to my right and Gale (and looking at me she said, "that is Johnny's twin sister"), you sit on the other side of father and the rest please sit in a circle." When all were properly settled, Mother Bow said, "Father, have no fear, tell it just as it was, we can take it." With that courageous remark the road was well paved. I methodically recalled for them how Johnnie came down with scrub typhus, how he successfully battled the first stages of the fever, how he gradually began to mend, even visibly improved, and how we all rejoiced gratefully. Also, I told them that Lori, the R.N. and I prayed with him every night, how he would never go to sleep until we said night prayers with him no matter how much dope they gave him. More, I assured them that nurse Lori stood and watched over him like a huge, mother guardian archangel. Yes, "Johnnie definitely was out of the woods" we all thought, I told them, until that terrible, fateful day.

Slowly and painfully, I reconstructed that fateful Sunday when we were bombed, described the terrible deaths in the huge fox-hole, and how I finally got home to my unit about 1:00 AM. I carefully told them that the rumor seeped through the jungle back to my unit, long before I returned, namely that it was I their chaplain who was killed in the fox-hole. I gave them the terrible reaction of my people, and the total astonishment and joy they experienced in seeing me alive: All except Johnnie Doe. Indeed, the terrible news was the straw that broke the camel's back. No amount of praying and pleading with Johnnie could bring him out of it. No, not even the tremendous spiritual help of Nurse Lori. He did reach up and (his final effort), asked to be baptized with a beautiful grin. I did it all by heart for I had done it hundreds of times the months before and many times since. I was almost glad when he went into a coma, for as clear and honest and compassionate as were our tears, we did not want to add to his suffering. I told them that I had made a solemn promise that sometime, somewhere, someplace, I would find you, his parents, his twin sister and all the family, and tell you all about his parting for a better world and a better life. I now have fulfilled that promise. I halted for a full minute and finally said, "Now Bow family, is there anything else you would like to know?"

The mother stood up, and as she did, I thought she stood ten feet taller than the empire state building. She said, Daddy and children I am completely satisfied. Let us go home and live our lives, as Johnnie would want us to. Our prayers have been heard. Johnnie died in the arms of a Catholic Chaplain, he is in heaven."

For years I still kept in contact but one day, I got a letter from Phil, the son-in-law. He was absolutely in his glory. Said he, "Father, Mother Bow died, but not before she asked to summon a Catholic priest to help her die. In her dying breath, she left this message... "I am going home to heaven with Johnnie."

As I read this story for the first time, I couldn't help but wonder how many mothers, fathers, sisters and brothers never got to hear how their loved one died. How many never heard the last words they ever uttered? Did they face the next world bravely or did they die trembling in fear? Fr. Kilian knew that these questions haunted the family members of every one of the soldiers who had paid the ultimate price for freedom. His words seemed to bring a sense of finality to the family, enabling them to move forward with their lives. That is why he was so committed to relaying as many of these tender stories as possible to the surviving family members.

Chapter 19

Civilian Life

When Fr. Kilian's new supervisor in Europe first reviewed his personnel record, he commented, "Would you kindly introduce me to this second Christ who rated a 5.9?" [1] (The highest rating that could be achieved was 6.0). After meeting with Fr. Kilian, he promised him that if he completed 28 missions or "revivals," he would earn a rating of 6.0, as well as a ticket home. To the supervisor's surprise, Fr. Kilian completed all 28 missions, and subsequently was discharged from the Army.

After a series of temporary assignments which included a spell with a mission house in Ft. Wayne, IN, Fr. Kilian was appointed "Superior of Religious Students" at the C.PP.S. Seminary in Collegeville, IN. Fr. Kilian was joined by two of his cousins from Kansas, Fr. Boniface R. Dreiling, Assistant Professor of Physics, and Fr. Marcellus Dreiling, Assistant Professor of Mathematics. Like Fr. Kilian, both were well over six feet tall, and very athletic. They were also baseball coaches for St. Joseph's college, which also offered a more traditional curriculum for non-seminarians. [2] The presence of both in the C.PP.S. Order and at the college is a testament to Fr. Kilian's ability to recruit young men to the priesthood.

His students from St. Joseph's still warmly remember Fr. Kilian. Fresh out of the military, he expected and received obedience and respect from the young seminarians and undergraduate students. He was not especially sympathetic to "whiners" or complainers after witnessing the deprivations and sacrifices that his young soldiers had endured. Yet, he always had time to listen and offer spiritual guidance. His wartime experiences, wisdom and his eloquence made him somewhat of a revered figure on campus.

One young student at Brunnerdale High School seminary in

Canton, Ohio, Harry Allagree, recalls a mission he attended, and the powerful impression left upon him by one of the priests.

"Our retreat master was Fr. Kilian Dreiling, C.PP.S. He had two other brothers (a reference to Fr. Kilian's cousins) who were priests in the community. Fr. Kilian had been an Army Chaplain in World War II. Quite a dramatic speaker, he graphically alluded to the horrors of Dachau during one of his talks. According to my notes his talks reflect a very traditional Catholic view of the world and of the priesthood. There is heavy emphasis on avoidance of sin at all cost, a sort of 'do-it-yourself-salvation,' and I notice the repetition of the fact that we needed to be 'men.' At the time, I thought Fr. Kilian was one of the best preachers we'd had." [3]

Fr. Kilian also made a strong impression upon another seminarian from this period, Fr. Albert Reed.

"Fr. Kilian was the rector at Xavier Hall when I was in college at St. Joseph College, Rensselaer, IN in 1947. He helped me a lot during my seminary days. He also gave us our annual retreat when we were students. He was a great speaker and Retreat Master." [5]

After three years as Superior of Religious Students and Religious Instructor, Fr. Kilian was again assigned to the Mission Band at Our Lady of Good Counsel in Cleveland, OH on September 1, 1951. Two years later he was assigned to Precious Blood Church in Fort Wayne, IN still a crusading missionary. This assignment lasted another two years. [4]

Throughout Fr. Kilian's life, he demonstrated a powerful gift for recruiting talented young men for the priesthood. It was obvious to those who encountered Fr. Kilian that he thoroughly enjoyed being a priest, and there was something very compelling about his own sincere, unwavering faith. The Rev. Robert L. Conway recalls how Fr. Kilian recruited three young men from the same parish for the priesthood.

"It was in January of 1941 that Fr. Kilian and another Precious Blood priest gave a two-week mission at our parish in Roseville, MI. Of the four high school boys who served those days, the next fall three of us entered Precious Blood seminaries and twelve years later we were ordained. Subsequently, a younger brother of mine and two other boys became Precious Blood priests.

"All of this was due to Fr. Kilian's taking an interest in us youths. Occasionally we would see him as he visited one of our seminaries." [6]

Fr. Thomas Beischel explains how Fr. Kilian cleverly suggested that entering the seminary was a "no-risk" proposition.

"I owe my vocation to Fr. Kilian. I visited him at St. Joseph College in 1949. I was 23, and myself a veteran of WWII. He said, 'Tom, give it a try. You can quit anytime for the next 8 years. Otherwise, when you are 78 (my age now) you will say, "I wonder if I should have been a priest?" Give it a try.' And so I did. I entered the C.PP.S. on August 1, 1949; ordained a priest on June 1, 1958. I have been a happy priest, and I thank Fr. Kilian almost every day." [7]

Eventually, the near-constant travel schedule of missionary life caught up with Fr. Kilian. In October of 1955 he was finally assigned to a more "stationary" assignment, that of Pastor of St. Michael's Church in Marywood, OH. Another aspect of his assignment was to be the Director of the C.PP.S. shrine at Marywood. For nearly three years, Fr. Kilian ministered to his local "flock" while simultaneously attending to the spiritual needs of the thousands of pilgrims who visited the shrine to the Blessed Mother.

It was at this point that Fr. Kilian, in the prime of his life, would suffer from a series of illnesses that would seriously threaten his life, dramatically affecting the pace at which he would be able to perform his sacred duties.

In August of 1958, Fr. Kilian entered St. Rita hospital in Lima, OH and learned that he had stomach cancer. The doctors removed his gall bladder, duodenum and most of his stomach. The prognosis in 1958 for someone with internal organ cancer was not very encouraging. Most of Fr. Kilian's colleagues assumed that he would not live very much longer. However, Fr. Kilian would once again defy the odds.

His convalescence was at first slow, but by March of 1959 Fr. Kilian was able to assume the role of Chaplain at Saint Mary Academy in Silver City, NM. This was a significantly less stressful and strenuous position, which allowed Fr. Kilian more time to reflect on a great deal many things. He now had more time to record some of his rich experiences on paper.

He was now 51 years old and had already lived an exciting, and what would be considered by most, a very full life. It would have been easy at this point, to simply kick back and retire. After all, most people would assume that at Fr. Kilian's current age and state of health, his most productive years were behind him. What was he now to do with the remaining months, or if fortunate years, that God granted him?

Fr. Kilian was not yet ready to live his life through the rearview mirror. It did not take an active mind like Fr. Kilian's long to find new causes to drive him forward. A timely letter from a distant relative in far-off Siberia would trouble him deeply, and would awaken from within Kilian a deep passion that would move him to action. [4]

Fr. Kilian during a visit with one of his sisters in 1946.

In 1953, Fr. Kilian visited George Rummel and his wife Ruth, who snapped this endearing photo of Fr. Kilian "horsing around" with two of the Rummel children, Bill (age 2) and Dorothea (age 4) (Hamilton, Montana). Fr. Kilian always had a great rapport with children.

Fr. Kilian prepared breakfast for all of the 92nd reunion attendees at his residence, which he called his "Little House on the Prairie." (August 1974)

The first reunion of the 92nd Evac. Hospital lifted the spirits of all in attendance as evidenced by the expressions on the faces of these attendees standing in front of Fr. Kilian's home (August, 1974). Pictured left to right (top) Bill Ahern, Fr. Kilian, Joseph T. Smith, (middle) Dr. Niemeir, Nurse Mildred Shellheimer, Dr. Nigg, Nurse Jean Kelly, Mrs. Nigg

Fr. Kilian and his nurses shared a special bond. (Indianapolis reunion, 1983)

The 92nd nurses presented this painting to Fr. Kilian as a remembrance of their days together in the Pacific. An image of Fr. Kilian is surrounded by images of Owi Island (top center), a tent chapel (center) and other camp images. The painting was done by nurse Margaret (Westbrook) Dickason.

In May of 1986, Fr. Kilian Dreiling celebrated his 50th Anniversary of his ordination at Carthagena, Ohio. On his left are his last two living siblings, sisters Armella (middle) and "Flitz."

A great gathering of friends and family were present to help Fr. Kilian celebrate his 50th anniversary as a priest, including members of both the 92nd Evac. Hospital and the 239th Combat Engineers. Both units traded stories after the ceremony.

Fr. Kilian electrified and delighted all in attendance at the 1991 92nd Evac. Reunion in Louisville by appearing in his class A uniform. Most of these veterans of the Pacific Campaign had never seen Fr. Kilian so elaborately attired.

Fr. Kilian and George Rummel entertain the crowd in Louisville, 1991.

At the 1993 92nd reunion in Orlando, the ranks were thinning. Fr. Kilian was unable to attend due to one of his bouts of ill health.

The Last Reunion: In 2002, only 11 veterans of the 92nd were able to make it to the reunion in Hamilton, Montana, hosted by the children of George Rummel (by then deceased). Pictured left to right (front row) Nurses Betty Spindler, Frances "Brownie" Larson, Betty McCully, Anna "Sammy" Coe, Jean "Kelly" Reed. (Back row) Jack Hall, Ben Brown, Joseph T. Smith, "Whitney" Choyeski, Mel Buscher, Lloyd Lambert.

This image of Fr. Kilian captures the depth of his facial expression. Of the photo he wrote, "It does not flatter me but I think it is great-true."

Fr. Kilian relaxes in his room in Carthagena, Ohio as he is interviewed for a local newspaper article about his years as an anti-communist lecturer.

In December, 1996, Fr. Kilian Dreiling was laid to rest with full military honors at St. Charles Seminary in Carthagena, Ohio.

Today, Fr. Kilian's grave lies in a quiet corner of the Priest's cemetery at St. Charles, alongside those of over 60 former military chaplains from the C.PP.S. Society. Sadly most of their incredible stories are buried with them.

Chapter 20

The "Red-Fighting Priest"

Fr. Kilian had a distant relative that somehow managed to survive the Soviet concentration camps and was finally able to send a letter to the Dreiling family in Kansas. In the letter, Fr. Kilian learned of the slaughter of his relatives and fellow Volga Germans under the Soviet regime. On August 28th, 1941, Joseph Stalin had abolished the Volga-German autonomous Republic. Some 379,000 Volga-Germans were deported to the frigid wastelands of Siberia and Central Asia, the memory of their beautiful villages and democratic enclave totally obliterated. Those that did not die along the tortuous journey were all but exterminated in the concentration camps. [1]

As the "Cold War" between the United States and the Soviet Union deepened, Fr. Kilian began to study the communist philosophies of Marx and Hegel. He saw a need for an educated voice, to step forward and speak up about the evils of communism. He would soon become one of the fiercest warriors of the Cold War. By combining his knowledge and his family's experiences in Russia with his own post-war experiences on the front lines of the Cold War in post-WWII Europe, Fr. Kilian became a formidable foe of communist sympathizers and advocates.

His strategy was simple. "My purpose was to educate people on the principals and philosophies of Karl Marx," Fr. Kilian once said. "I am a firm believer that education will take care of many problems. We are rational human beings, and we should appeal to the higher faculties of man. It's not an easy way, it's the difficult way" [1]

By speaking the truth eloquently, as only Fr. Kilian could speak it, he began to attract a significant following. At one time, he estimated that he had a following of some 60,000-80,000 college students. Newspaper articles tabbed him the "Red-Fighting Priest."

He also attracted the attention of the communists. The saga of the Volga Germans, and indeed the entire scale of the Soviet Gulags and concentration camps were not widely known by Americans at this point in time.

"It was a forbidden thing to mention," Fr. Kilian said later in a 1980's newspaper article. "I was the last leaf on the last limb of the tree. The great danger with Americans is that they just don't believe. I had a lot of threats, but that's part of it. It's exciting, thrilling." [1]

It was indeed exciting enough to warrant Fr. Kilian protection from the F.B.I. at one point.[2] The communist governments obviously considered Fr. Kilian Dreiling a serious threat. His lectures were not meant to entertain, but were a serious educational forum. Sometimes Fr. Kilian would lecture with notable or famous people like the Princess Garangia of Romania. Although he met with considerable skepticism at first, he said that gradually more people became aware of the threat of communism.

In Fr. Kilian's eyes, there was something deeply disturbing about the communist ideology. It was antithetical to everything he believed in and held most dear. It was a Godless and dehumanizing ideology that viewed organized religion as a threat, the "opiate of the people."

"They use Marxism as a tool," Fr. Kilian once said. "They began by saying they would protect the laboring man, but look at what they've done. They say human nature can be changed so that a mother will give up her child to the state as easily as a tree surrenders its fruit to the pickers. Gradually it will evolve; it's just a matter of time because Marxism goes contrary to human nature. Property, human rights, equality, no one can destroy them." [1]

Back in 1982, Fr. Kilian correctly predicted the fall of communism, some 8 years later. He said in an article for the local Wakeeney, Kansas newspaper that the Soviets' involvement in Afghanistan would be the "straw that breaks the camel's back." "That," he said, "was instrumental in keeping the Soviets out of Poland." [1] History has proved that Kilian's prediction was quite accurate. While Fr. Kilian's contributions to the downfall of communism may not have been as instrumental as those of another "Red Fighting Priest" from Poland named Carol Wojtyla, Fr. Kilian no doubt played a key role in helping to open the eyes of the American people to the evils of its ideology.

There is an interesting postscript to the story of Fr. Kilian's battle with communism. As much as Fr. Kilian detested the communist ideology, he is reminded in this next story that his Christian faith does not allow him to hate those who practice it.

"Some years ago when I was in quasi-retirement at St. Charles, I came to know and love an old, saintly brother. He was the embodiment of all that was holy, kind, pleasant and cheerful. Standing in bold relief was his ever-ready smile. A smile that would gain credibility because it was accompanied with a profound bow whenever he passed you in the hall.

"One busy day I accidentally met him while on an urgent errand. When I came close to him he slowed down his pace and looked at me intently. 'Father,' he said, 'Would you do me a favor?'

" 'Certainly brother, what is it?' I asked.

" 'Would you say a Mass for me?' He reached into his pocket and handed me a washed-out dollar bill. I looked at the offering and said, 'No, brother, I will gladly say the Mass without an offering.' His reaction was swift and visibly reflected on his face. 'Father,' he said, 'the widow's mite was the smallest of all the contributions put into the treasury that day, but Jesus said that she gave more than all the rest together.'

"I felt roundly rebuffed. I quickly took the offering and attempted to walk away with haste. But he stopped me with another question.

" 'Don't you want to know who it's for?'

" 'Yes, brother, if you wish.'

"Calmly but firmly he said, 'Say the Mass for Stalin. You know he just died.'

"I was speechless for a moment. Inwardly, I was reluctant, even chagrined. What Stalin had done to my relatives in Russia over years and years rose before me like an insurmountable mountain. A second time he sensed my reluctance and resolved my scruple.

"Gently he led me down the hall and said, 'Father, Jesus came to earth to shed his Precious Blood not so much for the angels and saints, but for poor sinners. Stalin you know was the greatest of sinners and must therefore lay claim to God's greatest mercy and kindness.'

"It took me three days to chew on brother's words. Only after I reconciled myself to the wisdom of this simple, holy brother would I offer the Mass. And never did I offer Mass with such fervor as the Mass I finally offered for Stalin.

"More importantly, I now find it easier to offer Mass for people like Saddam Hussein, all because a humble brother aroused in me a basic important Christian doctrine in the simplest, every day language."

As I write this, it is only a few short weeks after the fall of Baghdad and the evil regime of Saddam Hussein. I cannot help but think that the lesson Fr. Kilian learned back in 1952 is just as relevant for those of us living in the 21st century.

Chapter 21

"Truly, Does any Brutal, Costly War Ever Come to an End?"

One of the hidden costs of any war is the psychological impact that the very real and terrible images, indelibly stamped in the minds of the combatants, have upon the survivors. As noted earlier in this book, Fr. Kilian suffered tremendously from the haunting images that used to come to him in the middle of the night. However, he was able to turn his own sufferings into compassion for others, who were similarly afflicted.

Sometimes the images would be triggered by events, a familiar song, or for no reason at all. Many years after the war, in the late 1950's, Fr. Kilian was shaken when he learned of the tragic fate of a young soldier who had once been one of his altar boys. Fr. Kilian was a dear friend of the young man's family. As Fr. Kilian states, "all names are fictional" in this next story.

Among the finest families of the Parish (Holy Trinity in Louisville, KY), was the Fox family. Father and Mother, sons and daughters all pitched in to do their duty (when the parish church burned down). They were the seasoning of the soup of the parish. But the joy of the Fox family, like that of millions of other families, came to a sudden and shocking dead-end. World War II broke out.

Both sons enlisted immediately. Sean, the counterpart of his typical Irish mother, became an ace pilot. He went down over the English Channel early in the war. His body was never recovered. Peter, the counterpart of his yodeling, Tyrolian father, was captured in Saipan in 1944. For years, the military notification, "missing in Saipan," remained unchanged.

It was because I dearly loved the people of Holy Trinity, I returned periodically for a visit, a funeral, or a wedding. It was on one such occasion that I readied to detrain, when a quiet gentleman next to me held the morning paper in my face. He asked, "Do you by chance live in this city?" I replied, "No, I am just returning to visit old friends." Then, flashing the headlines in my face he said, "Would you by chance know this lad who was taken prisoner on Saipan?" I looked at the headline in utter disbelief and consternation. It read, "The saga and fate of Peter Fox." I literally gasped, "Mr., that boy and his brother were my most faithful altar-boys when I was Associate Pastor in their parish. He said, "Reverend, I am sorry, but in that case you will want to read on."

Yes, Peter and his platoon were ambushed on Saipan. Thanks to the typical dense jungle, all managed to escape except Peter. Securely hidden in the thicket, his friends watched from afar. The enemy took Peter, stripped him to his skin as was their custom, and then strapped him to the trunk of a tree. With a rousing war whoop, they danced in brutal glee and hate. Waving their sabers, they systematically took turns dismembering him. One would chop off his right foot, the next his left. A third would sever his right leg at the knee, while a fourth would hack away at his thigh. They continued this relentlessly, even severing both arms. Finally, they decapitated him, crowned a stump of a fallen tree with his head for the vultures to devour. However, under the total cover of jungle darkness, his friends reverently gathered the dismembered body and buried it in a shallow grave, then quickly fled to a safer distance deeper in the jungle.

This terrible episode remained a secret for 13 years. But one of the platoon members could resist the strain no longer. For him, it was either "telling it all," or sliding into insanity. He called for a reporter and "told it all." Unfortunately, the family was not forewarned. Both parents died of prolonged grief within months of each other.

However, there was also a noble and a sacred aspect to this horrible crucifixion. <u>Not unusual at all among soldiers</u>, Peter had wrapped a rosary around his right hand that not even death nor the enemy could disentangle. Yes, the enemy destroyed his dog tag, but they would not dare touch his rosary.

It is highly improbable, if not totally impossible, that the bones of Peter will ever be discovered, but if they are, his remains will be identified not by his dog tag, but by the rosary that will still cling tenaciously to the bones of his fingers.

As an ardent son of St. Gaspar, with a profound devotion for the Precious Blood of Jesus, I ask, "Should we not be forcefully driven, yes, even impelled by the spirituality of the Precious Blood to share all aspects of Peter's crucifixion with our confreres and acquaintances? I think so!

For consideration: There are striking parallels between the crucifixion of Jesus and the execution of Peter (Fox). Jesus died in obedience to his father's request, namely to redeem mankind through the shedding of his blood. Peter died in obedience to his patriotic conscience and died for his God and countrymen. Jesus shed his blood through the five wounds. Peter shed his blood through a thousand and more saber wounds. Both were led to the slaughter like a lamb, without a whimper or a protest (he never whimpered or pleaded for mercy I was told). Jesus was crowned with thorns. Peter crowned the stump of a tree with his decapitated head. Jesus was nailed to the wood of the tree. Peter was strapped to the wood of the trunk of a tree. Jesus' body was laid in a stranger's tomb. Peter's dismembered body was secretly buried in a strange country, indeed a foul, infested jungle. To Jesus we attribute the condescending words, "Father, if it be possible, let this chalice pass me by, but not my will but thy will be done." Of Peter we say, "Greater love than this hath no man that he lay down his life for his friends." For Jesus, not a bone was broken. For Peter, hardly a bone remained unbroken.

To be sure, infinite support came from their undivided love and faith in their Heavenly Father. But tremendous support came also from someone at the feet of both trees, the gentle, tearful support of the Blessed Mother. To Jesus she was physically present. To Peter she was present in the beads of his rosary wrapped around his hand, a presence very, very real.

And may we not presume that the Blessed Mother will do (the same) for the Fox family and millions of other suffering families for whom this war is still an ongoing, brutal, costly crucifixion- indeed, a ruthless, never-ending holocaust?

Our rewarding consolation resides in the hope that knows not despair, a hope that is as infinitely enduring as the infinite love of God himself for his creatures. With unwavering trust and faith and love, we truly profess to all the world that Peter, now cleansed in His Blood, will like Jesus, at the appointed time, rise from the dead and sit next to the Father and His Son. For where the head is there also must be the members of the body of Jesus.

This we staunchly believe; this we preach in season and out of season. In it we place our hope. For this grace, we pray perseveringly and passionately; yes, with the bold impact of fire and brimstone.

Events like those described in this last story are incomprehensible to the rational mind. Natural reactions upon hearing such a depressing tale would be shock, horror, or even avoidance of the topic altogether. How do we begin to understand a mindset that condones making "sport" of the dismembering of another human being? While debating whether to include this story in a book about Fr. Kilian Dreiling's life, I asked myself, "Is it really necessary?" The answer came quickly. "Fr. Kilian must have thought it was necessary, or he would not have recorded it."

It is only through the relaying of such stories that the sacrifices of young men like "Peter Fox" will ever be known or appreciated. We should never forget them. Fr. Kilian believed this very strongly. This is the best reason I can think of for him to commit these tragic and graphic stories to paper.

Psychologists tell us today that the very act of writing down disturbing or troubling thoughts and images can help us face our fears. It is actually a form of "behavior therapy." After years of carrying around such disturbing images in his head, Fr. Kilian finally decided to record them. No doubt, it helped him come to grips with his own demons.

However, Fr. Kilian did not just stop at recording these images. He made a concerted effort to try and make sense of them. While he clearly understood that war is a terrible waste of precious life and resources, he also observed that it brought out the very best in a great many people. He found in the sacrifices of young soldiers something very sacred. He was also able to make a connection between their sacrifices and those of Jesus Christ. In their blood he saw the Precious Blood of Jesus. While Jesus redeemed us, the dying soldiers earned our freedom. In this way, the sacrifices of Jesus became very real and very tangible for Fr. Kilian. He witnessed them nearly every day, and he wanted us to remember them always.

Chapter 22

The Good Shepherd

From 1959 until 1965, as Fr. Kilian's health improved, he was given assignments of increasing responsibility, with correspondingly higher workloads. His first assignment after returning from cancer surgery and sick leave was as chaplain of St. Mary Academy in Silver City, NM. [1]

Then, in October of 1965, Fr. Kilian's career would enter a new and much more stable phase. At the age of 56, Fr. Kilian the globetrotting missionary would once again become a parish pastor. This would be the longest continuous assignment of his career, lasting nine years and culminating in his first "retirement."

Over the course of these nine years Fr. Kilian, as pastor of Christ the King parish, would leave an indelible impression upon the community of Wakeeney, Kansas. By the time he retired at the "Sundowner Lodge" in Wakeeney, he was "One of the town's most loved and respected citizens" according to the local newspaper. [2]

One of Fr. Kilian's qualities that endeared him not only to his Catholic parishioners, but also to those of many faiths, was his genuine respect for the sincerity of others' beliefs. Fr. Kilian explained his ecumenical beliefs in a sermon that he gave during an Army reunion in 1993. [3]

"A truly sincere and honest non-Catholic friend of mine recently asked me this provocative question. Said he, 'Padre, you are a Catholic, more, a Catholic priest. How do you justify your dealing so kindly and understandably with all denominations of other beliefs, races and cultures?'

"My answer was simple, instant, quiet but forceful; yes, quiet as dropping a thought on a feather bed but as forceful as the Amazon at its lowest depth. First and foremost, we are all creatures of a 'one, true

God' no matter by what name we call him or worship him. Also, we all are created according to the image and likeness of this God, and God being who he is, infinitely kind, merciful and just, did this out of pure unadulterated charity. Accepting this premise as self-evident, we declare that it is totally inconceivable that God <u>will not respect</u>, care for, and love any of his creatures who honestly and sincerely believe what they believe, or <u>do</u> what they consider equally honest and correct. True, God, I, or you may not agree with our neighbor in every detail, just as he may not agree with our total thinking, but if God respects and loves him (our neighbor) for his sincerity and complete honesty, then who am I to contradict God's will?"

These same ecumenical beliefs, practiced and perfected as an Army Chaplain, would endear Fr. Kilian to the entire Wakeeney community.

While many aging people become cynical and bitter about the rebelliousness, disrespect and moral decline of younger generations, Fr. Kilian always had a tender spot in his heart for young people. "I have a tremendous feeling for the young people" Fr. Kilian would say, "I hate to see our youngsters ruined by drugs. There was a time I could go 20 hours a day — I could go out and find the youngster — but not anymore." [4]

Believing that religious education and spiritual missions were powerful tools in the battle for the hearts and minds of the parish youth, Fr. Kilian saw the need for classroom facilities for their religious education. He organized the construction of a $120,000 youth center (in 1971 dollars), and had the facility paid off within three years. He celebrated the occasion with a "mortgage burning ceremony," followed by a dinner for 200, cooked by Fr. Kilian himself.

At one time, thirty CCD teachers taught 229 youngsters about Christ every Wednesday evening. Fr. Kilian personally oversaw the curriculum, and participated fully in the program. He was proud of the fact that there were rarely more than three our four students absent on any given evening.

Borrowing from the teachings of Jesus, Fr. Kilian often used references to nature in his homilies. He developed a beautiful orchard, which included apples, pears, peaches, cherries, nectarines and apricots. These trees he would compare to God's good and righteous people who "bear much fruit for others."

Once Fr. Kilian recalled the very first funeral he ever conducted for a young child. He fretted many hours about what to say to the girl's grieving family. In his homily, he compared the beautiful little girl to a flower in God's garden. "Sometimes God desires to pick his most beautiful flowers before they're withered," he said. [5]

Fr. Kilian confided that he loved to hear the confessions of young children. He would laugh as he described the occasion when a little boy corrected him about giving him a penance that was not severe enough. Apparently, the boy had confessed the same sin on another occasion and Fr. Kilian had given him a stronger penance. [5]

Christ the King parishioners gave Fr. Kilian very high marks for his sermons. Drawing from his wartime experiences, he always seemed to be able to select just the right story from his rich repertoire for every occasion. A priest friend of Fr. Kilian's, Fr. Joseph Nassal, described his preaching style. "Kilian was a preacher with fire in his belly and fire in his bones. When he preached, this fire could warm the hearts of those who heard him. Or, like John the Baptist, his fire could scorch a few souls." [5] People at Christ the King church actually looked forward to hearing the Sunday sermons.

During this time, Fr. Kilian also saw the need for Sunday services at a local resort, Cedar Bluff Lake. He held Mass out at the lake every Sunday for "the weekenders" at the lake for the last six years of his assignment in Wakeeney. He also helped organize Protestant services at the lake.

Another one of Fr. Kilian's passions was his year-round clothing drive for the poor people of Mexico. "The whole community" he said, "brings clothes because they know that they really go to the poor." Fr. Kilian, along with members of the Wakeeney community, gathered the thousands of pounds of clothes and trucked them to Mexico annually. [2]

During an assignment of nine years, lifelong bonds of friendship are developed. Two of Fr. Kilian's best friends in Wakeeney were Mark and Agnes Pfannenstiel. Fr. Kilian soon found out that he and Agnes were related. Fr. Kilian's grandfather (Kuhn) and Agnes's grandmother (Gerber) were brother and sister, and lived as Volga-Germans in Russia.

Agnes recalls fondly the first year of Fr. Kilian's assignment to Christ the King.

"He found out I was his cousin. He had a special name for me that his family had for my Grandma Gerber in German that translated to "Gerber-Aunt." One day he said, "Agnes, would you teach CCD this fall?" To which I replied, "Father, I can't teach. Mark and I never were blessed with children, only a lot of nieces and nephews."

"Would you at least try?" Fr. Kilian replied.

I said, "Under one condition. I can quit if I feel I can't do it." I taught three weeks and Fr. Kilian asked, "How did it go?"

"Father, I'll never make a teacher," was my reply. Fr. Kilian informed Agnes that there were other things she could do.

"So I was known as the "film lady" for all 13 grades for ten years. He also gave me the job of Parish Secretary, which I held for as long as he was pastor of Christ the King." [4]

Agnes refused to accept any compensation for her services. She was happy to be of service to her parish community. Like Fr. Kilian's mother of the same name, Agnes today draws from her own "storehouse of memories," and cherishes the time that she and her late husband Mark spent with Fr. Kilian. Fluent in German, Agnes and Fr. Kilian would often converse in their "first language," sometimes singing German songs.

Fr. Kilian was not particularly fond of "book work," so before he talked Agnes into becoming the Parish Secretary, he would ask her and Mark to come to the rectory and count the collection. His ongoing bribe was, "If you come over and count the collection I'll cook supper for you two!" This bribe proved very effective thanks to Fr. Kilian's remarkable cooking skills. "His favorite treat was Russian meatballs and rolls," recalls Agnes. "I'd bet there isn't one of his family or many of his friends that hasn't at some time or other eaten his famous meatballs and rolls." [4]

Fr. Kilian would hide the Sunday collection in his washing machine, under the dirty laundry. One Sunday, he had to "come clean" about his hiding place. He had forgotten about the collection money, and had run the washing machine with the Sunday collection still inside. The money came out OK, but the checks were destroyed. As a result, Fr. Kilian had to stand up in front of his parishioners and announce sheepishly, "If you gave a check last Sunday, would you please reissue another?" He wasn't worried because he knew that every one of his parishioners would do as he had asked. [4]

Another parishioner, Mrs. Irene Garmann, fondly recalls how Fr. Kilian frequently enlisted the services of her husband Ed to repair his car, build shelves or perform household repair jobs. Once Fr. Kilian asked Ed to install a window fan in the kitchen to help get rid of his cooking odors. On one occasion, Fr. Kilian was confiding in Ed about how tired he was running around and saying Masses for all the surrounding parishes. Ed told Fr. Kilian he should slow down and refuse to say some of the Masses. Fr. Kilian's response was instantaneous. "Ed, I never married and I never had a wife to nag me, and I don't want to be nagged now." [6]

It was while Fr. Kilian was pastor at Wakeeney that he survived a near-fatal auto accident. He had borrowed Agnes and Mark's pick-up truck, and had visited his sister Armella in Cannon City, CO bringing with him, a load of clothes for the poor. On his way home, he had overloaded the truck with Colorado rock "for the front of the rectory," blew a tire and rolled the truck in a ditch. Fr. Kilian suffered many bruises and cuts and spent time recuperating in an Eads, KS hospital. Agnes and Mark Pfannenstiel rushed to visit him in the hospital. As soon as Fr. Kilian saw them he began to cry and said, "I'm sorry about your truck." They assured him that the truck could be fixed, but reminded him that *he* on the other hand, was *not* replaceable. Fr. Kilian's good friend Dr. Hamilton flew to a nearby airport in his private plane and took Fr. Kilian back to Wakeeney with him. [4]

As Fr. Kilian's health began again to fail him, he decided to retire from active parish ministry. "Physically, I'm worn out." Fr. Kilian said in the summer of 1974. "I should go out and visit my old people, but in most cases I'm sicker than they are." [2]

Fr. Kilian's retirement party was a huge affair, and was attended not only by the 200 families of Christ the King parish, but by the entire community of Wakeeney. After travelling for three months, Fr. Kilian described his plans for retirement.

"I plan to do some writing, a lot of reading, listen to a lot of good music and hope to raise a garden and tend to the orchard- along with visiting my friends." [2]

Before retiring to the Sundowner Lodge in Wakeeney, near his dear friends, Fr. Kilian wanted to follow through on a wonderful idea that he had been hatching for some time. It had been nearly thirty years since he said good bye to the young men and women of the 92nd Evacuation Hospital in the Philippines. It was the last time that he had seen most of them. After the war, all everyone wanted to do was forget the hardships and sacrifices, and get on with life. Now however, Fr. Kilian felt that enough time had passed to allow the healing of old wounds. He longed to again see the faces of the young men and women with whom he had labored so hard to save so many young lives.

Fr. Kilian reckoned that Wakeeney, Kansas was the perfect spot for the first reunion of the 92nd Evacuation Hospital. After all, it was located in the center of the United States, and it possessed a population of willing accomplices, ready to do his bidding.

As Fr. Kilian pondered how he might accomplish the daunting task of contacting each and every one of the 92nd veterans, now scattered across the United States, he naturally contacted his former tent-mate and "scrounging partner" Ed Gray. Ed was now living in San Diego. Ed's first reaction was, "Why in the world would you want to have a reunion in a God-forsaken place like Wakeeney, Kansas?"

Fr. Kilian's reply was swift. "Ed, Wakeeney is the perfect place for the reunion, and I can assure you that because I am here, it is NOT God-forsaken." [7]

Chapter 23

Reunion

In September of 1974, in Wakeeney, Kansas, they began to arrive. They came in small groups from every corner of the United States, all converging on the little prairie town of 2,800 residents. They came by plane, train, by bus and by car.

For most of the Wakeeney residents, this would be a Labor Day weekend like no other. Many, like Agnes Pfannenstiel, had helped Fr. Kilian organize, plan and prepare for the small invasion of 92nd Evacuation Hospital army veterans. Dozens more would help prepare and serve the meals and refreshments decorate the reception hall and clean up afterward. It was a testament to their love for their retiring pastor Fr. Kilian, that members of the community donated all of the funds and labor necessary to host these events. After everything that Fr. Kilian had done for their them, they were happy to go the extra mile to make this event special for their beloved pastor. [1]

Along with his parish friends, Fr. Kilian enlisted the services of several of the 92nd veterans, in tracking down as many of the veterans as possible. In the end, they were only able to contact slightly less than half of the original 255 doctors, nurses, officers and enlisted men. However, most of those contacted were able to make the pilgrimage to Wakeeney.

It had been 30 years since they last ate and slept together; 30 years since they had huddled together, hiding from enemy air raids. Would they now be the same people? Would they even know each other now, after all these years? Any doubts or anxieties the 92nd veterans had about seeing each other again were quickly dispelled.

Awaiting them in Wakeeney was an entire community, ready to welcome them with open arms, and to facilitate a carefully crafted series of events designed to make this one of the most memorable weekends of their lives. Their thoughtful "Padre," Fr. Kilian, of course, carefully orchestrated all of this.

Spontaneous celebrations began as soon as the guests started registering at the Sundowner Lodge. After hugs and introductions, the veterans had a lot of catching up to do about how their lives had unfolded these last 30 years. Inevitably, the story telling began. The good food and drink were made all the more enjoyable by the many comparisons to the dismal living conditions they had endured together in the Southwest Pacific.

They enjoyed looking at each other's pictures, movies and slides. A wall that had been set aside for the veterans to post their war era pictures became a popular gathering place. A highlight was the viewing of rare movies from their days on Owi Island, including footage of one of the famous 92nd baseball games. [2]

It soon became apparent that there was a beautiful spirit being rekindled among the 92nd veterans. This same spirit, which had been present 30 years ago, had gone almost unnoticed until now. Only now, with hindsight filtered by time, could they really recognize it and appreciate it. They had not just survived the war, they had labored together in miserable conditions to save thousands of lives. Together, they had made their corner of the world a better place. Old grievances were now forgotten.

Noticeably absent was any distinction between the officers and the enlisted men. During the war, the U.S. Army's "no fraternization" policy and better all-around benefits for the officers were sources of resentment for the enlisted personnel in every branch of the service. Now, all class or rank distinctions seemed nonexistent. All that was left now was an appreciation, love for the best people each of them had ever known, and they did not want it to end.

Here is a typical example of the kind of humorous banter that was nearly continuous over the reunion weekend. It is transcribed from a tape recording made during the actual Wakeeney reunion. They are the words of Fr. Kilian reflecting back upon several of the 92nd veterans. [3]

"Thurman, Thurman, I was sleeping soundly and someone was shaking me and I woke up. I was on a litter. Thurman said, "Padre, can I talk to you?" I thought, "Thurman, you can't have any marital problems 6 or 7,000 miles away," and he said, "You know Padre, I have to tell you, I just had to tell you. I have 5 or 6 uncles, (I forgot how many), and he said, "Would you believe they were all hanged for thievery?" I said, "Thurman, when did they start this horse thievery?" "Oh, when they were 15 or 16 years old." And I said, "When were they hanged?" "Oh, when they were about 75 or 80 years old," he said."

"So the next night, about 3:00 in the morning, there was Thurman again shaking me and I said, "Thurman, what is it this time?" He said, "I'm worried. My conscience bothers me. My mother wasn't quite sure whether one was hanged or shot." (loud laughter follows). I said, "Thurman, you can come once more and you will be shot."

"Kelly (nurse Jean Kelly), I better not start, I just want to thank you. It's always the women that tell you the nice things. The men are mean." (laughter)

"I can't say anything about Gray (Supply Officer Ed Gray) because it's a matter of the right hand and the left hand. No matter what he stole, if he did it with the right hand I did it with the left hand."

"Smitty (author's father) and Ahern (author's uncle Bill Ahern) have always just been real good friends of mine. I just feel sorry for their wives, they don't know..."

"Willy (nurse Althea "Little Willy" Williams), the thing I know best about you is, you always cheated for the enlisted men. But that was only in baseball right?" (Willy was the best pitcher on the 92nd softball team).

The spirit was infectious. Not only did it manifest itself with the spouses and guests of the veterans, the local Wakeeney residents exhibited it as well. "Welcome flags" greeted the veterans from almost every boulevard. Many were surprised to hear "No charge" from local pharmacists filling their prescriptions or by local restaurateurs when ordering meals. No one wanted to go to sleep, but eventually all had to give way to the demands of nature. [2]

At 9:00 AM on Saturday morning, Fr. Kilian personally cooked breakfast for the entire group at his small house, situated directly behind the Sundowner Lodge. He called it his "Little house on the

Prairie." They feasted on Fr. Kilian's famous homemade bread, rolls, sweet rolls, donuts, and gallons of delicious coffee with rich, homemade cream. [2]

The highlight of the weekend came on Sunday at the memorial service. Former Nurse Jean (Kelly) Gallagher provides a vivid description of the event in a letter sent to all of the members of the 92nd a few weeks after the reunion.

"An overcast sky greeted us Sunday morning. In fact, it was raining. But by now nothing could dampen the spirit of the 92nd. En masse, the gang filed into father's church, Christ the King, for the 10:00 AM Mass. And again, the hospitality of his people was there. The front pews were reserved for visitors. It was also Fr. Dreiling's last Sunday in his parish before his retirement. It was great having our very own "Padre" once more. For him, I am sure it must have been a greater day still, seeing before him faces that long ago he saw under grass chapels, and on rough wood benches, or boxes or logs. After Mass and a quick breakfast, we once more returned to Father's church for the planned Memorial Service at 1200 hours.

"Parishioners had hastily vacuumed the church after the 10:00 AM Mass so as to have it immaculate for the Memorial Service. It was. For the second time that day the church was packed to capacity. The service opened properly and thoughtfully. A letter was read from one of our greatly respected nurses, who beautifully reflected the sentiments both of those present, and more particularly, those absent. It awakened us to the stark reality that those who were not present in body were most certainly with us in thought. Father opened the Memorial Service by reading a letter from a mother (Mrs. Harris) of one of our members who gave his life at San Fabian in 1944. After the sermon, Father read the names of all our departed comrades, followed by the playing of taps, high in the tower of the church. The entire Memorial Service was devastating. There was not a dry eye in the church... Truly, it is difficult to put into words the tremendous impact of the Memorial Service." [2]

It was not long before everyone began making plans for another reunion. Now that they had found each other again, they could not simply let the spirit die. They were a family once more. A certain sadness was felt for the many members of the 92nd who had missed this wonderful experience. However, a concerted effort would soon be made to round up the "stragglers." Those who did make the pilgrimage to Wakeeney were rewarded for their efforts by the renewal of old friendships, and the initiation of brand new ones. These beautiful relationships would last for the rest of their lives, and true to their word, they would continue to hold reunions every 2-3 years until 2002.

All of this happened because of one man's vision. The same man, who watched over the 92nd like a "mother hen" for 2-1/2 years in the South Pacific, somehow knew that they needed him again; that they needed each other again. To each of them, Fr. Kilian Dreiling was a true friend. He personally hugged every, last one of them before they headed for home, and in so doing, Fr. Kilian expanded his circle of friends almost exponentially. For soon there would be "mini-reunions," regional reunions really, and Fr. Kilian would attend most of them, (he was after all "retired" now).

After the first Wakeeney reunion, excited letters began arriving addressed to "92nd Evac. Hospital Headquarters" in Wakeeney. A newsletter was sent to all known members and their friends, and in the first issue, several descriptions of the reunion were published.

Wrote one, "Padre, you transplanted the spirit of Owi to Wakeeney by blotting out the intervening years, and intensifying it 1000 times." Another said, "It (the reunion) was the greatest thing that happened to me in my life." Another letter reflected upon the healing effects of time. "Our reunion was perhaps the greatest neutralizer I have ever studied. It took from the past the best, sloughed off the worst, and then ended with the very best of today." [2]

In the years to come, Fr. Kilian would come to know and love the families of the 92nd veterans, including their sons, daughters and grandchildren. At a time when most retired priests are witnessing their friends and family dying off, Fr. Kilian would be saying special Masses, attending weddings and offering his wise advice and counsel to a new generation of his growing "92nd family." He truly became "re-energized" by this new chapter in his life.

Before my father attended the first Wakeeney reunion, I do not recall him ever even mentioning Fr. Kilian Dreiling. After the reunion however, Fr. Kilian would stay at our house on many occasions, usually saying Mass with us in our own home. In addition to making the Mass much more personalized, it had the added benefit of not requiring us to dress up and battle for parking spaces at the church. Even as a 16-year-old, I thought this was cool. We came to love "Fr. Dreiling", as we knew him, as a revered member of our extended family.

After the reunion, in October of 1974, some of Fr. Kilian's influential friends were able to persuade then President Gerald Ford to send the following letter, addressed to "Father Dreiling" on official White House stationary. The letter was a total surprise to Kilian.

"Dear Father Dreiling:

"Through the courtesy of Senator Griffin I have learned of your recent retirement. I am pleased to have this opportunity to let you know of my personal appreciation for your long and dedicated service to our country.

"Your distinguished career, both in times of peace and war, has been an outstanding example of devotion to others. I hope you will always look back with pride on the service you have given and the special contributions you have made. I am sure that I speak for our fellow citizens, especially the members of the 92nd Evacuation Hospital, in expressing heartfelt thanks.

"You have my warm best wishes for continuing happiness and fulfillment in the years ahead."

Sincerely,
Gerald R. Ford

Chapter 24

Keeping the Spirit Alive

The final 22 years of Fr. Kilian's life followed a somewhat cyclical pattern. Recurring bouts of ill health were followed by periods of rest, recuperation and "retirement." Upon recovery, Fr. Kilian would soon find himself in the services of the Catholic Church again, by now facing a serious shortage of priests. These assignments often consisted of assisting at small, outlying parishes close to home. In some cases, Fr. Kilian was called upon to oversee the activities of one of the C.PP.S. sites like the "Sorrowful Mother Shrine" in Bellevue, Ohio. [1]

Fr. Kilian describes how his activities are now largely contingent upon his physical condition.

"1982, by and large, has been kind to me. True, I had still another bout with death in early June, but in time managed to surface beautifully, decimate all derogatory predictions about my possible survival, and finally, to prove my determination, retrieved some fifteen pounds of the fifty that I had lost. I now look no longer like a skinned lizard. I look more like a skinned cat. Like Santa Claus — certainly not! But of much more value is one's frame of mind. Mine remains vibrant and ever hopeful." [2]

Fr. Kilian also kept up a brisk correspondence, the volume of which had increased exponentially after the first Wakeeney reunion. With more free time, he began to write down the stories that were contained in this book. Most of the stories he had retold many times from the pulpit. Now, X-Mas seemed to be the occasion which gave him pause to reflect, reach into his deep "storehouse of memories," and share his experiences with us all. Every year we, Fr. Kilian's friends and family, would look forward to receiving his X-Mas letter. With every letter, new adventures would unfold. Sometimes, these letters would combine wisdom with humor, traits that Fr. Kilian inherited generously from his mother. Here is an example from Fr. Kilian's X-Mas 1984 letter to his "flock."

"Somewhere in a footnote this account is recorded. The apostles were given a psychological aptitude test. Results: Peter, because he was willful, impetuous, arrogantly aggressive at times, a poor runner, a faulty fisherman, not to mention a 'denier,' surfaced a poor risk. The outcome of the eight hung in the balance. Thomas, understandably, was late but eventually came and passed the test by a slight margin. Judas, because he was a financial tycoon, a schemer, a shrewd operator, came up the only sure winner. History does invariably reveal the truth but unfortunately, often too late." [3]

In 1985 Fr. Kilian was plagued with blood clots in his left leg and was forced to use a cane. An altar boy asked him, "How come your legs are so weak and your jaw so strong?" "To this day," Father said, "I have not deciphered if he was prompted by innocence, brilliance or pure unadulterated mischief." [4]

The planning of the 92nd's reunions became an enterprise that occupied a great deal of Fr. Kilian's time and energy. In addition to the big reunions every 2-3 years, there were numerous, smaller reunions. Many of the veterans who could not or would not make the long journey to Wakeeney, KS or Denver, CO were able to travel the shorter distance required for these smaller get-togethers. In some cases, the 92nd veterans needed to go and seek out members whom no one had seen since the end of the war. Such was the case for "John Doe" from Kentucky.

In 1978, there was a mini-reunion in Columbia, KY. This provided a rare opportunity to track down one of the most well liked and lovable characters in the unit. "John Doe", as Fr. Kilian refers to him in the upcoming story, also had a nickname, "Jeep". Kilian wrote the following article for his local Trego County, KS newspaper about this occasion. I have taken the liberty of substituting "John Doe's" <u>real</u> nick-name into the story as "Jeep" has now passed on.

The Beautiful Ugly Stable

Out of respect for his real name, we shall call him "John Doe

(Jeep)." He lives in the hills of Kentucky, deep and dark as the waters of the Southwest Pacific. He is a genuine hillbilly; one that has never voluntarily left his native county. In other words, he has never left or crossed the county line since WWII. For the balance of this story, let us return to the first person or persons.

On Nov. 5th and 6th, 1978, a small segment of the 92nd Evacuation Hospital held a mini-reunion in Columbia, Kentucky. Columbia, I repeat, nestles quietly and humbly in the deep Southeast of Kentucky. Because Jeep resolutely refused to cross the county line, we, the mountain, traveled to Mohammed, Jeep. He had a stroke some years back, and is presently plagued with an affliction that somehow compels him to speak not only with his tongue, but with his arms and legs as well. However, his mind is absolutely aglow. Without a doubt, Jeep was the most popular enlisted man in the unit. He was never more than a private 1st class. He never did more than police the area and do K.P. (a "Yardbird" in 92nd lingo), but he was truly the seasoning of the 92nd Hospital soup.

During the last two weeks, I visited six doctors who belonged to the same outfit. As soon as I told them we had a mini-reunion in Columbia, each in turn and individually, and automatically asked, "Tell me Padre, did you see Jeep?" Before the sixth could complete his question, I promptly replied, "Yes, I saw Jeep." I or we had not seen Jeep since 1945; in other words, since VJ Day.

This gang, perhaps 40, took turns visiting Jeep. The pattern remained constant. We drove ten to fifteen miles to the next county, left the black-top road, veered to the right, traveled still another three miles on a trail road along-side a dry stream completely hidden by huge trees and undergrowth. The trail came to an abrupt end. On foot, we forded the stream. There on the side stood a typical hillbilly shack. It was no more than 20 feet long and perhaps eight feet wide. The stoop was piled high with firewood, the yard littered with discarded furniture, buckets, frying pans, kettle etc.. etc... In bold relief on the stoop sat Jeep, ready and anxious to welcome us. He had aged terribly, naturally! He spoke falteringly. He was unbelievably dirty. His shack could not have been cleaned in 20 years. He himself we agreed, had not had a bath in ten years, perhaps twenty. His only supply of water was a five gallon bucket, periodically replenished by rain from the roof. There was no running water, but he did have one small bulb in his living room. Never! Never! Had I seen a house or a person so utterly neglected.

As we neared the stoop, someone said, "Jeep, do you know who this is?" Quite indignantly, he replied, "Ah certainly well do. He is our Padre." With that he clinched my legs and would not let go until we finally left. Tearfully, he shook hands with the rest, but always held tight to my legs with one arm. Eventually, he called for silence. He reminded the group how I had one time saved his life. During a bombing, his foxhole was totally covered (see story chapter 9). Only the top of his carbine still showed. I rushed over and dug him and his friend out. I had totally forgotten about it. He had not. All the while we took pictures, recalled, answered a million questions, but most of all enjoyed this truly wonderful man who contributed so much to the esprit de corps of our unit.

Without signal or warning, he belaboringly got to his feet, and pleaded with me to come into his castle. He wanted badly for me to have a remembrance of him. He offered me his most treasured possession; a bookmark with the Good Shepherd on top and Psalm 23 written or printed below. He paged throughout his Bible, but because of his affliction, his efforts were fruitless. I said, "Jeep, what precisely are you looking for?" He replied, "The Lord is my Shepherd." With that he handed me the Bible, and almost immediately I found the bookmark. With almost holy dignity, and I sensed also with sadness, he pressed the bookmark into my hands with these words, "Padre, I so want you to have this. It is the only treasure I value in my house. Please accept it. You saved my life." Naturally, I accepted it, and not without tears.

Because we had a great distance to travel, I said, "Jeep, we just have to move on." Once more, with the greatest of effort, he rose to his feet and to the occasion, pleaded for silence and said, "No, No! Padre, not yet!" And addressing the entire group he solemnly announced, "First, our Padre will pray with me." All fourteen stood in a circle, held hands while I recited loudly and clearly, Psalm 23. I finished the first verse and in the wake came a command, "Halt!" With Jeep still clinging to me, he raised his eyes to heaven and with the greatest love and sincerity prayed, "Good God bless our Padre." I proceeded with the second verse and at the end, he again called a halt. Once more he raised mind, body and soul to heaven and said, "Good Lord, bless all these good friends who so kindly came to see THIS NO GOOD, THIS NOTHING, THIS DOG IN THE WOODS." Again I would continue reading, but again he would interrupt me and simply look to heaven and shed bitter, but grateful tears. Over and over, he thanked us, and always with the thought, "Why did you come to see this nobody, this nobody, this dog in the woods?" Before I finished the Psalm, all fifteen were in tears, but happy tears because we all felt that we had done a good deed. We visited and cheered Jeep, who though only a Private 1st class, contributed perhaps more to the well-being of the unit than I, their chaplain.

Then suddenly, and clearly and loudly came the thought. If Jeep was filthy, dirty, even repulsive, and if his shack was even more dirty, and more filthy and even more repulsive, could it have been that the stable of Bethlehem was equally dirty, filthy and repulsive, but that the soul of Jeep was as truly beautiful, kind, grateful, deeply loving as the soul of the Christ Child that lay in the dirty, filthy, repulsive stable of Bethlehem?

We left. All of us hugged him, wished him well and loved him intensely because inside that dirty, filthy, repulsive stable dwelt a soul as genuinely beautiful as the soul of the Christ Child.

My father and mother were two of the fourteen who witnessed this event and prayed with Jeep. They recalled that the stench was almost unbearable, yet they described it as an extremely spiritual moment; one they would never forget. Jeep was loved by his comrades for his simplicity, his sincerity and because of his genuineness. He was a man who was small in stature, but big on pluck. He would fight at the drop of a hat, but everyone knew that if trouble was brewing, Jeep was a guy you would want standing next to you. He would cover your back. [5]

Isolated from human contact for most of his life, Jeep possessed the ability, perhaps more acutely than most of us, to see Christ in others.

In Fr. Kilian, he saw the light of Christ burning so brightly that he could hardly bear to see it leave his presence. It must have been quite a humbling experience for Fr. Kilian. Here was a man he had not seen in 33 years clinging to his leg, begging him to stay and pray with him. It is clear from reading this story, how much Fr. Kilian's soldiers loved, revered and respected him. These feelings only seemed to intensify with the passage of years. There were many more reunions, but after the second Wakeeney reunion in 1977, the number of attendees began to diminish, and the number of names on the roll call of those who had passed away increased.

Fr. Kilian also attended some of the reunions of the 239th Engineering battalion. He had sailed to the South Pacific, and had participated in the first two island landings with this unit. As he had with the 92nd, Fr. Kilian renewed old friendships and began many new ones with members of the 239th Engineers as well.

It is possible that all of the reunions and celebrations finally caught up with Fr. Kilian. In December of 1980, he voluntarily checked himself into a rehabilitation program for Catholic clergy suffering from alcoholism, proving that he too was human. By December 23rd however, after three weeks in the program, Fr. Kilian felt good enough to send the following, buoyant letter to my mother and father. He had just received a letter from my parents asking for his prayers for my sister's husband, their son-in-law, who was suffering from severe alcoholism.

"Dear Smitties:
"Received your Xmas card, note and report. Please note that I entered the Guest House (A rehabilitation center for Catholic Priests in Lake Orion, MI) Dec. 1st. I saw so much of late on alcoholism that I decided that in no way will I let myself reach that level. And promptly admitted myself to the program. It was the smartest thing I have done in forty years. The program runs for fully three months, but because of my unbelievable progress, I may leave even a month earlier. But I am not pressing this point.
"The place, the program and the minds that run this

program are absolutely, fantastic. Some of the greatest minds in the country run and teach here. Now that I am well along, I decided that I would want the program even if I were a saint. It is 3/4 spiritual and 1/3 chemical. In less than three weeks I was converted into an absolute new creation. It is unbelievable. My whole outlook on life has taken on a new perspective. Many of my powers (natural) now function beautifully and easily. I am calm, at ease, relaxed etc..etc... The approach is most sophisticated, but thorough...The final step in the program is to share your knowledge with still another victim...

"Tell me, would your son-in-law resist help? You see, it is absolutely amazing how they will accept help from another alcoholic, but will resent the same help coming from a non-alcoholic. If you feel that I could be of any help let me know. Give me his address etc. The program is naturally based on the 12 steps of the AA, but goes far beyond the AA program. Also, it has a cure and it is infallible if we pursue it seriously and faithfully for severe nervous depression, drugs etc.. I don't know when I've learned so much, and profitably as these last three weeks. I learned that my thirst for knowledge has not diminished. On the contrary, it is as sharp as ever. My counselor has to hold me back constantly. I still want to start everything today and finish it yesterday.

"I am fortunate beyond measure. I walked into this place much as a duck walks into water. I resented nothing. I accepted everything, and retained a cheerful demeanor. One of my counselors nick-named me "Smiling Dreiling." Another said yesterday, "Kilian, you are so delightful, I hate you." I said, "Mr. Taylor, that you love me is the rose on the bush. That you hate me is the thorn on the bush." He literally burst at the seams. But I did give them a hard time. I accepted nothing unless I could intellectually sift it through my brain. Frankly, I gave them a hard time but they are equal to the task." [6]

Fr. Kilian's positive attitude and early intervention were responsible for his remarkable recovery. Unfortunately, Fr. Kilian's offer of help would come too late to be of any assistance to my sister's husband, who passed away at the young age of 34, four days after Fr. Kilian wrote the letter. Alcoholism was the primary cause of death.

The 92nd reunion in 1985 took place in Denver, CO. This was a good meeting place for those members west of the Mississippi. Most of the doctors were from the Colorado area and some were still in practice there.

After another memorable reunion, a total stranger approached Fr. Kilian. She had worked behind the front desk of the hotel that hosted the reunion. This story explains beautifully, how infectious the love and friendship of the 92nd truly was. Fr. Kilian, extremely moved by the incident, included this story in his Xmas letter of 1985.

"As about ten of us stragglers passed through the lobby on our way to the airport, a lady who was a total stranger to me, working behind the counter, called to me and asked to speak to me personally. Exactly, she said, 'Father, may I speak to you, please?' Hesitatingly, I retraced my steps. With eyes already swimming with tears and lips quivering she avowed, 'Father, do you realize that you are the most adored man on earth?'

"Totally taken by surprise and not knowing what to say, I simply stammered and stuttered. Without further adieu, she forged ahead, 'Father, your unit just adores you. Don't you know that?' Long after I captured my breath and my senses, I managed to say, 'Thank you lady for your beautiful vote of confidence, but do you realize how dearly I love them?'

"Given that impetus she launched into a veritable tirade (sic), 'That,' she said, 'was most conspicuously obvious. Never have we, the staff, seen love handled and exchanged so beautifully, freely, genuinely and sincerely as during your reunion. All through the week, love, compassion, concern, interest in each other, was your sole and exclusive priority. It was beautiful! We have many, many reunions here in our Inn, but we have never seen anything like your reunion. You carried love for each other, not only on your lips but in your hearts. Your sudden outbursts of warmth, love and affection, like the rumblings of a distant thunder, increased and decreased but always recurred with greater intensity and beauty. Truly great! All of us here in the lobby not only recognized it, but enjoyed it immensely, and most of all, we, without you knowing it, freely shared in your lusty and lively camaraderie. And now, we would like to thank you one and all.'

"Because she spoke so freely and especially so openly (as all strange Catholics do in meeting a strange priest), I presumed that she was a Catholic and said quite honestly, 'Lady, you must be a Catholic?' With an angelic smile that embodied all the grand good of both the Old Testament and the New Testament, she replied, 'No Father, I am Jewish. But anyone who could not detect the depth and beauty of your friendships and rejoice in it, and share in it, should never have been born. We are a better people for witnessing your mutual love and kindness.' "

At the 1991 reunion in Louisville, KY, Fr. Kilian had a surprise for his friends. Only one couple knew about his little secret: my parents. At the very beginning of the reunion banquet, My father stood up and belted out, (as only my father could do), "ATTENTION!" The hall became instantly quiet. Dad began speaking again, "Folks, there stands outside, a dear friend of General MacArthur and he is most anxious to once more, meet the members of the 92nd." [5]

With every neck in the room craned to the front of the hall, Dad opened the door, and in walked Fr. Kilian Dreiling in his class A uniform. The uniform still fit perfectly, and Fr. Kilian's face beamed from ear to ear as the entire room erupted in an outpouring of emotion. Fr. Kilian described what happened next.

"The reply was spontaneous and immediate as thunder follows lightning and equally forceful. My nurses you see, and many of our visitors had never seen me in my class A uniform...only in fatigues. Never in all of my 84 years have I been kissed as often, and warmly, as in the hour that followed my appearance. In other words, the mustard seed of love, planted 50 years ago in the Pacific, had now matured and grown into a veritable tree where the angels from heaven now share in it's branches, their love with us earthly people." [7]

Chapter 25

Embracing Old Age

During the reunion years, Fr. Kilian accepted as part of his mission, the helping of his 92nd family to "grow old gracefully," resolutely, gratefully and accepting of God's will. Many of the sermons from his Memorial Services over these years carried this theme. As fewer and fewer veterans showed up at each ceremony, the roll call of the missing veterans at the Memorial Services became longer, and longer.

Fr. Kilian was a man who was always learning. Throughout his life, he had the ability to step back and look at situations from new perspectives. Thus, he was able to treat setbacks and difficult situations as learning experiences. He saw many older people become disheartened, bitter or grumpy, and he refused to become one of them. He was committed to doing whatever he could to help prevent his 92nd family from becoming downhearted as well.

Sharing his wisdom and comforting perspectives with the veterans through his homilies at the reunions, and through his prolific correspondence, Fr. Kilian also left a record of his "recipe" for growing old gracefully. Here are a few of these gems of wisdom.

"Heavenly Father, look kindly on all members of the 92nd Evac. Hospital, both those present and those absent. Support them generously, encourage them and lay your hand of blessing upon each and everyone. Grant to all the good fortune to accept old age gracefully, yes, even cheerfully. Console the sorrowing and the sick, and all those who suffer great grief. All this we ask and much more as you are definitely merciful, forgiving and generous. Amen."
(92nd Evac.Hospital reunion, Indpls., IN, Sept. 1983)

"Members of the 92nd Evac. Hospital, little did I realize or even suspect that 35 years after we parted, the shadows of our experiences

continue to follow me and you. There is scarcely a day, certainly not a week, but what some shadow overtakes me. Some are good, others sad. The fact is life. The important thing is that we accept this fact, and at times it is not easy. I'm an old man, 73, and the older I get, I really and truly believe, the more sense I get. I am very, very slow to condemn. In fact, I refuse. But on the other hand, over the period of 35 or nearly 40 years, I have learned one thing. Be kind, be forgiving, be loving."
(92nd Evac. Hospital Reunion: September, 1980, Pueblo, CO)

"But now come to the basics. I have developed a psychology since my retirement. Incidentally, retirement to me is the greatest thing on earth. I now sit back and think, and I have come to a psychological principal that all are as good, as kind, as compassionate, as holy, as the good that we see in our neighbor. It's a basic principle that I had and learned only after I was retired. On the other hand, we are evil, as wrong, as the evil we see in our neighbor and in ourselves, and no better. The wonderful thing, and take it from the old patriot, the wonderful thing about the 92nd , rests in this. We have consistently, perpetually, constantly been able to say, 'I see the good in my fellow member because I see it and accept it with joy and cheerfullnes.' We are what we are."
(92nd Evac. Hospital Reunion: Indpls., IN, Sept., 1983)

"Then there's one more thought...You know I was in my trailer house for two solid months. Never came out, double pneumonia. That's when I decided 'That's it.' I rebelled. I resented the fact the other coworkers would be working and here I was not out of my room for two solid months. One day, I was especially at outs with God and there was nothing I could do. He could be just as stubborn as I, so I went and laid down on my bed. I reached down and brought out my Bible and automatically I read, not knowing what was coming up. I read, 'Whether you eat or drink or sleep, whatever you do, do it for the honor and glory of God.' I said, 'There is the answer. My body is tired, my mind is tired, my knees are tired for sure, but there was the answer.' After that I said, 'Look, I lie down, I sleep, I rest my body, I rest my soul, I rest my heart, and then doing it for the greater honor and glory of

God I even get a bonus. Here I rest the body, the soul, and God gives me a reward, even for being lazy, if you have the right intention.'

"So when I hear of anyone having sorrow, whatever, I always pray to the Good Lord to give them that understanding. It took me almost 75 years to learn it. It's absolutely shameful that I had to be that old to learn that lesson."

(92nd Evac. Hospital Reunion, Indpls., IN, Sept., 1983)

By 1989, the theme of coming to grips with the loss of so many loved ones had become increasingly important. Fr. Kilian selected the following poem for the back of the program during the '89 reunion in Hayes, Ks.

Should You Go First

Should you go first, and I remain
To walk the road alone,
I'll live in memory's garden, dear,
With happy days we've known.
In Spring I'll watch for roses red,
When fades the lilac blue,
In early Fall when brown leaves call
I'll catch a glimpse of you.

Should you go first and I remain,
For battles to be fought,
Each thing you've touched along the way
Will be a hallowed spot.
I'll hear your voice, I'll see your smile,
Though blindly I may grope,
The memory of your helping hand
Will buoy me on with hope.

Should you go first and I remain,
To finish with the scroll,
No length'ning shadows shall creep in
To make this life seem droll.
We've known so much of happiness,
We've had our cup of joy,
And memory is one gift of God
That death cannot destroy.

Should you go first and I remain,
One thing I'd have you do:
Walk slowly down that long, lone path,
For soon I'll follow you.
I'll want to know each step you take
That I may walk the same,
For some day down that lonely road
You'll hear me call-your name.

Fr. Kilian's last residence was St. Charles Seminary in Carthagena, Ohio, the same place where he began his days as a young seminarian at age 13. He had "retired" there three times altogether. Once in 1979, in 1983, and finally, in May of 1992. [1] Here are some of Fr. Kilian's reflections upon his first retirement there in 1979.

"My life of retirement at St. Charles is absolutely, peaceful. I do not recall ever being so content with the world, myself and my neighbor as there. True, since '78, June, I have not been home one single week-end, but it is a glorious feeling to come home after the week-end job, enter my suite of rooms, close the door and say, 'This is my castle. I am home.' My quarters are both ample and practical. I have three huge windows that face west. As I gaze westward, the eye sees as far as it can travel. Before me lie in absolute repose, vast fields of corn, beans, hay and woods. Between and betwixt, and among these lush fields, church steeples stand out in bold relief and command the eye ever heaven-ward. The entire panorama can become breathtaking, especially in the winter time.

"There are in all, nearly one hundred members in this far-flung complex, and upon arrival I knew all for 55 years on down. In fact, it has been my home-base since 1924. I know not only every nook and corner, indeed, I recall well every nook and corner in which I carried on mischief all through my twelve years of studies as a student." [2]

Even at this late stage in Fr. Kilian's life, he was still making new friends and leaving lifelong impressions. During one of Fr. Kilian's stints as a "fill-in" pastor for one of the many local community parishes, St. Anthony's in St. Anthony, OH, he befriended the parish secretary, Mrs. Barbara Goffena with the following words.

"Barb, is your office warm enough and would you like a cup of coffee?"

Mrs. Goffena goes on to explain how Fr. Kilian was able to leave a lasting impression upon her during those short six weeks.

"From his daily homilies at Mass and our conversations in the office, I felt as if Jesus himself was there speaking to me. People who came into the office also left feeling the same way."

I fondly remember the occasion that I visited Fr. Kilian at St. Charles while staying at a nearby hotel on a business trip. The year was 1986. By this time, the sprawling complex no longer served as a seminary, but as a retirement home. There were many empty rooms.

Fr. Kilian could not have been more delighted to welcome me. He was always genuinely interested in the lives of his friends. Although his body was frail, his mind was unbelievably sharp for an 80-year-old man. He had a small hot plate for cooking, a refrigerator, a pantry, and many books in his room. He seemed extremely content. He warmed up some turtle soup, which he had made the day before (I do not know where he got the turtles). Hesitantly, I tasted this new "delicacy," and was pleasantly surprised. It was absolutely, delicious.

We talked about family, his days at the seminary, the war years, and eventually the conversation came around to the topic of his writings. I urged Fr. Kilian to allow someone to compile his writings into a book. "They are too good *not* to be shared with others," I said. "That is for someone else." He told me. At the time, I remember thinking that "someone else" would certainly find his writings and someday publish them. If no one else picked up the mantle, then perhaps I could follow through for him.

However, even heroes like Fr. Kilian cannot live forever. After spending several months in the St. Charles infirmary, Fr. Kilian called my father in early December of 1996. He said, "I think I have used up all of my nine lives. I am in such pain, please pray that God will come and take me. I'm afraid too many people are praying for me to live." [3] Fr. Kilian finally passed away on December 6, 1996. He was 90 years old. Appropriately, the wife of one of his 92nd veterans was at his side.

Fr. Kilian's friends arranged for a 21-gun salute at his gravesite.

The chapel at St. Charles was nearly full, as many of Fr. Kilian's friends and family made the journey to Carthagena in order to pay their final respects to their dear friend. It was not easy to say goodbye to a man who had given so much strength to others but we knew Fr. Kilian would suffer no longer. He had labored long and hard in the fields of his Master, and we were consoled that he would now be able to taste the fruits of his labor.

Fr. Kilian's body now resides in a place of honor, alongside those of dozens of other former military chaplains from the C.PP.S. order at the St. Charles cemetery in Carthagena, OH. Each granite headstone is identical and laid out with military precision: perfect rows, perfect diagonals. During the warm weather months, crisp, American flags point out the graves of the military chaplains. Bronze plaques, attached to the flags highlight the conflict in which each priest served: WWII, WWI, The Korean Conflict, Spanish American War, and even one veteran from the American Civil War.

History will likely not remember the names on the headstones: Fr. Klement Falter, killed during WWII's early stages in North Africa, Fr. Aloys Selhorst with whom Fr. Kilian celebrated V-J Day, and Fr. John Wilson, who survived three years in Japanese prison camps. They now lay side by side, having served their God, their country, their order and their fellow man with great distinction. They may have taken part in different wars, different theatres, or faced different enemies, but their mission was always the same. The chaplains from the Society of the Most Precious Blood have helped make our world a more beautiful place. As Joe Gerber so eloquently describes in his letter thanking Fr. Kilian for his spiritual direction and guidance, "We will not be judged solely by what we did or did not accomplish in our own lifetimes, but by the impact we have had on the lives of those who survive us as well."

In January of 1997, Fr. Kilian's good friend Joe Nassal wrote a tribute to his friend in the province newsletter, "The New Wine Press."

"A few weeks after he moved to Carthagena, I received a letter from Kilian in which he told me he was not in the house more than a few hours when people approached him to give a retreat. He was also summoned that day to the infirmary at the request of another priest who was dying. When Kilian walked into the room, the priest said, "Thank you, Jesus, you have answered my prayer. Now that Fr. Kilian is here he will help me die." Kilian prayed with him for more than an hour and found a reason why he moved to Ohio: to help others make that journey from life to death, to life again."

"Now, Kilian has made that same journey. As he did so many years ago when he stood on the shore of the great ocean and washed the blood of soldiers from his hands, his body, and saw their blood mingling with the waters, so now Kilian stands on the other side of the shore. May we wash our hands, our hopes, in the memories and stories of Father Kilian and so come to a deeper understanding of what it means "to be redeemed in the blood of Christ."

Fr. Kilian wrote the following poem sometime during the war. It was published in the Grove Gazette, Quinter, KS in 1945. A young Kansas soldier, Wendall Robert, stationed in Europe, received this poem from his parents. He cut it out and saved it for 52 years. It was again published in the same paper on May 21st, 1997, five months after Kilian's death.

"In Memory"

Let me take you for a moment to a tropical isle at war,
Where the soldier sings ever onward, to do his daily chore,
When the enemy shows no mercy, and we give none in return,
Where our thoughts turn ever homeward, and our loved ones yearn.

Where the bullets are thick as raindrops, as we draw our
    labored breath,
And one error in judgement may cause a sudden death.
There a forest of white crosses marks the bones of those who died,
And I hear the murmur of their voices in the thunder of the tide.

I hear my friends there whisper to their comrades at their side,
As I bow my head in sorrow for the souls who took the ride.
There my prayers rise to Our Savior that he let them rest awhile.
Here's some things I heard them whisper from their great,
    eternal night,

While the tears streamed from the eyelids in the early morning light.

Have we kept the men's traditions, have we done our duty now?
Will there be peace in heaven as there seldom is on earth?
Why are our loved ones crying as they gather round the hearth?
Were we fighting for our freedoms, or someone's worldly gain?
Will we ever rest in comfort after all this war and pain?
Will the sword become the plowshares while the guns are red
    with rust?
Have we ended wars in future, though they molder the dust?
Will the gold star in the window be enshrined within the heart?
Will the honor that they pay us fade, grow dim and die?
Will the purple heart they gave us be worn with tears and pride?
Can the gleaming piece of metal take our places at their side?
Will they learn their folly from us that there's death in every strife?
Will they ever learn the value of a single human life?
Can we help them live their future, avoiding sorrow and pain?
There's the question, yours to answer, where you dwell
And the future of this world they have left to you and me.

Let us break down isolation, do our part for world-wide peace.
When all nations see their folly, then these frightful wars will cease.
When we make each man our brother, and believe, "Thou shall
    not kill."
Then we'll be building a great future, and shaping the Lord's Will.

Epilogue

When our time on this Earth is finished the impact we have made, good or bad, does not end. Fr. Kilian's legacy is that of a man who not only made this world a better place while he lived, but through the lives of those he inspired, continues to do so today. As I prepared to take the manuscript for "Our Padre" to the publisher, I received the following letter, reinforcing that Fr. Kilian still lives in the hearts of all who knew him. Almost immediately, I recognized that it would make the perfect epilogue to the story of Fr. Kilian's inspiring life.

Letter to Fr. Kilian from His Friend Joe Gerber

As I sit here and reflect on my life and the man I have become, many people come to mind. Many people that have loved me guided me and formed me, but only a few people can be credited with starting me down the right path. Only a few can be called my mentor. Fr. Kilian is one of those people. He is a friend that I will ever be grateful for, that I will always be conscience of for bringing me to the truth. He is a seeker of truth and a lover of truth. He lived *truth* and he *was* truth.

As I sit here and reflect, I must mention that I am not merely doing a daily reflection on my life, or just recalling good thoughts of a kind person or priest. I am in the middle of a five-day discernment retreat in preparation for receiving the sacrament of Holy Orders into the Diaconate. This is a serious time in my life, after four years of study and spiritual formation. As I get closer to this great day where the Holy Spirit will mark my soul for all eternity with the seal and graces of this Holy Sacrament, I remember my call to this vocation. I must say that it was not one event that brought me to this point, but a series that were each needed in their proper order to achieve its ends.

God brought Fr. Kilian into my life when I was a young boy. I lived in Colorado and we would come to visit my Aunt Agnes in Wakeeney, KS. Fr. Kilian had a gift of how to know people. He knew their hearts and loved them for who they were. I am convinced that he must have known from the moment he met me that I would be called into the service of the church, which he so loved. Although he treated everyone with the love and respect each person is entitled to, we shared a special, unspoken bond that only the people who share it can explain.

Over the years, we were able to continue this bond, strengthen it and bring it to its fullness. I received many special gifts from him, gifts that meant a lot to him and me. I realized that I was his family. Everybody was his family. When I was 17 years old, a time when most teenagers only think about having fun, I traveled with my parents to see him in Ohio. Another level of our relationship was born. A spiritual one started to make me realize my love for God and his Church. His support and prayers continued in my life as I was married and as I continued to be influenced by the right people and the right situations.

The last gift I received from Fr. Kilian was one of his stoles that he wore throughout his priesthood. The note said, "I thought you might like this whenever you consider becoming a deacon." It was put away for many years on a shelf with only an occasional thought of those words. He died, but his legacy, his prayers and his accomplishments are still living in the actions, minds and hearts of many. I am one, small project that he started among so many. He produced fruits beyond measure by just being, doing and living as Jesus commanded us to do from the one simple command; "Love one another as I have loved you."

The content of this book is filled with nothing but firsthand witness of this same kind of selfless giving and love. Many of the stories are humorous in nature, but with the seriousness of a mission that will not stop short of total giving of self; total love of neighbor.

When we pass on from this life, our bodies leave, but our soul remains until it is forgotten. Our works continue to either bear fruit or produce harm and evil. We are not to be judged by only what we accomplished while we are here, but by all that continues to be because of our lives as well. Fr. Kilian's fruit continues to be harvested daily and more rapidly than when he was alive. We must not forget this. If we are benefactors of that fruit, of that truth and of that love, we must carry it on so that our lives may have the same or better impact for ages to come.

I will kneel before the Archbishop of Denver, CO on June 12, 2004. As he lays his hands upon me in silence, I will be blessed to be in the same company as the holy men that have received this sacrament before me. I will remember my mentor, Fr. Kilian Dreiling, and I will know that his work continues, unforgotten by God, but unknown to so many. I will strive to be to some young child, and to all God's children, the person of Christ. In doing so, I am closer to living out my ultimate goal, a goal I know was achieved by Fr. Kilian; complete union with God.

Therefore, I owe my utmost gratitude to him, as do all those who knew him, and as do all those who did not know him but are reading about him now, perhaps for the first time. We owe him our gratitude for helping us see the world as it should be seen, for making us smile and for making us just feel good, for changing our lives for the better and for giving us each a greater chance of eternal salvation. Thank you Fr. Kilian. Your legacy lives in my heart and in the hearts of many for ages to come. I love you.

Soon to be Rev. Mr. Joe Gerber (Deacon Joe)

Bibliography

Chapter 1 "The Confession of 'The Beast' "
(1) From Fr. Kilian Dreiling's homily, 92nd Evac. Reunion, Indpls., IN, Sept., 1983

Chapter 2 "From Russia to the Windswept Plains Of Kansas"
(1) Fr. Kilian Dreiling's personal family records
(2) Most of the historical background regarding the migration of the "Volga-Russions" to the U.S.A. is derived from the book, "Conquering theWind", Copyright 1966 by Amy Brungardt Toepfer and Agnes Dreiling. Re-printed with permission of the American Historical Society of Germans from Russia (AHSGR)
(3) Excerpted from sermon given by Fr. Herbert Leinenberger's homily at the Mass of the Volga-German Centennial celebration at St. Fidelis Church, Victoria, KS, July 28, 1976.
(4) Oral history of Agnes Pfannenstiel, 2003
(5) Oral history of Fr. Kilian Dreiling
(6) Excerpt from brochure, "St. Fidelis Church," Victoria, KS, circa 1975

Chapter 3 "The Young Seminarian"
(1) Excerpted from "Missionaries of the Precious Blood, C.PP.S." brochure published in Carthagena, OH, August, 1987
(2) Letter from Elsie Schneider, May 11, 1998
(3) Excerpt from a homily given by Fr. Kilian Dreiling at a retreat, circa 1985
(4) Oral history of Joseph T. Smith
(5) Excerpt from brochure, "Shrine By the Little Lake", published at St. Charles Seminary, Carthagena, OH, circa 1985
(6) Oral history of Fr. Kilian Dreiling

Chapter 4 "A License to Save Souls"
(1) "Official Service Record" of Fr. Kilian Dreiling, C.PP.S.
(2) Letter from Elsie Schneider, May 11,1998
(3) "For God and Country, Book 1," Copyright 1993 by
     Fr. Paul Link, C.PP.S., "The Messenger Press," Carthagena,
     OH. (pg. 11)
(4) Excerpt from a sermon given by Fr. Kilian Dreiling at a retreat,
     circa 1985

Chapter 5 "A New Calling"
(1) "For God and Country, Book 1," Copyright 1993 by
     Fr. Paul Link, C.PP.S., "The Messenger Press," Carthagena,
     OH. (pg. 4)
(2) "For God and Country, Book 1," Copyright 1993 by
     Fr. Paul Link, C.PP.S., "The Messenger Press," Carthagena,
     OH. (pp. 99-100)
(3) "For God and Country, Book 1," Copyright 1993 by
     Fr. Paul Link, C.PP.S., "The Messenger Press," Carthagena,
     OH. (pg. 27)
(4) "For God and Country, Book 1," Copyright 1993 by
     Fr. Paul Link, C.PP.S., "The Messenger Press," Carthagena,
     OH. (pg. 98)
(5) Letter from Rev. Robert L. Connay, Feb., 2005

Chapter 6 "Off to War"
(1) "Official Service Record" of Fr. Kilian Dreiling, C.PP.S.
(2) Letter from Lou Weisgerber, August, 1998
(3) "For God and Country, Book 1," Copyright 1993 by
     Fr. Paul Link, C.PP.S., "The Messenger Press," Carthagena,
     OH. (pg. 75)

Chapter 7 "Hollandia: The First Invasion"
(1) Scrapbook of Dr. (Capt.) E.F. Pfile of the 92nd Evac. Hospital, containing newspaper clippings from the period 1943-45 from "The Denver Post"
(2) "For God and Country, Book 1," Copyright 1993 by Fr. Paul Link, C.PP.S., "The Messenger Press," Carthagena, OH. (pp. 84-85)
(3) "For God and Country, Book 2," Copyright 1993 by Fr. Paul Link, C.PP.S., "The Messenger Press," Carthagena, OH. (pg. 246)
(4) Oral History of Joseph T. Smith

Chapter 8 "The 92nd Evacuation Hospital"
(1) "Tales of the 92nd Evacuation Hospital," brochure printed from Sept., 1993 92nd Reunion at Orlando, FL, containing oral histories of veterans of the 92nd (pg. 4)
(2) "Tales of the 92nd Evacuation Hospital," brochure printed from Sept., 1993 92nd Reunion at Orlando, FL, containing oral histories of veterans of the 92nd (pg. 69-74)
(3) "Tales of the 92nd Evacuation Hospital," brochure printed from Sept., 1993 92nd Reunion at Orlando, FL, containing oral histories of veterans of the 92nd (pg. 72)
(4) "Tales of the 92nd Evacuation Hospital," brochure printed from Sept., 1993 92nd Reunion at Orlando, FL, containing oral histories of veterans of the 92nd (pp. 59-61)
(5) "Tales of the 92nd Evacuation Hospital," brochure printed from Sept., 1993 92nd Reunion at Orlando, FL, containing oral histories of veterans of the 92nd (pg. 73)

Chapter 9 "No More Easy Victories: The Invasion of Biak Island"

(1) Scrapbook of Dr. (Capt.) E.F. Pfile of the 92nd Evac. Hospital, containing newspaper clippings from the period 1943-45 from "The Denver Post"

(2) "Tales of the 92nd Evacuation Hospital," brochure printed from Sept., 1993 92nd Reunion at Orlando, FL, containing oral histories of veterans of the 92nd (pg. 15)

(3) "For God and Country, Book 1," Copyright 1993 by Fr. Paul Link, C.PP.S., "The Messenger Press," Carthagena, OH. (pp. 88-89)

(4) "Tales of the 92nd Evacuation Hospital," brochure printed from Sept., 1993 92nd Reunion at Orlando, FL, containing oral histories of veterans of the 92nd (pg. 49)

(5) Quote from 92nd Evac. Reunion, Wakeeney, KS, 1977

(6) FN: Information about Archie Roosevelt from web site "Archie Roosevelt, son of Theodore Roosevelt," (www.theodoreroosevelt.org/life/familytree/archive.htm), retrieved Aug. 24, 2004.

(7) Oral history of Joseph T. Smith

Chapter 10 "The Owi Island Campaign: A Different Kind of enemy"

(1) Oral history of Joseph T. Smith

(2) "Tales of the 92nd Evacuation Hospital," brochure printed from Sept., 1993 92nd Reunion at Orlando, FL, containing oral histories of veterans of the 92nd (pg. 16)

(3) "Tales of the 92nd Evacuation Hospital," brochure printed from Sept., 1993 92nd Reunion at Orlando, FL, containing oral histories of veterans of the 92nd (pg. 50)

(4) Scrapbook of Dr. (Capt.) E.F. Pfile of the 92nd Evac. Hospital, containing newspaper clippings from the period 1943-45 from "The Denver Post"

(5) "Tales of the 92nd Evacuation Hospital," brochure printed from Sept., 1993 92nd Reunion at Orlando, FL, containing oral histories of veterans of the 92nd (pp. 17-18)

(6) "Tales of the 92nd Evacuation Hospital," brochure printed from Sept., 1993 92nd Reunion at Orlando, FL, containing oral histories of veterans of the 92nd (pg. 76)

(7) "Statement of Service" record of the 92nd Evacuation Hospital, official U.S. Army records

Chapter 11 "The Invasion of the Philippine Islands"

(1) "For God and Country, Book 2," Copyright 1993 by Fr. Paul Link, C.PP.S., "The Messenger Press," Carthagena, OH. (pg. 189)

(2) "Tales of the 92nd Evacuation Hospital," brochure printed from Sept., 1993 92nd Reunion at Orlando, FL, containing oral histories of veterans of the 92nd (pg. 51)

(3) Oral history of Joseph T. Smith

(4) "Tales of the 92nd Evacuation Hospital," brochure printed from Sept., 1993 92nd Reunion at Orlando, FL, containing oral histories of veterans of the 92nd (pg. 22)

(5) "For God and Country, Book 2," Copyright 1993 by Fr. Paul Link, C.PP.S., "The Messenger Press," Carthagena, OH. (pg. 241)

(6) "For God and Country, Book 2," Copyright 1993 by Fr. Paul Link, C.PP.S., "The Messenger Press," Carthagena, OH. (pp. 189-190)

(7) "For God and Country, Book 2," Copyright 1993 by Fr. Paul Link, C.PP.S., "The Messenger Press," Carthagena, OH. (pg. 211)

(8) "For God and Country, Book 2," Copyright 1993 by Fr. Paul Link, C.PP.S., "The Messenger Press," Carthagena, OH. (pg. 272)

Chapter 12 "The Search for a Brother"

(1) "For God and Country, Book 1," Copyright 1993 by
  Fr. Paul Link, C.PP.S., "The Messenger Press," Carthagena,
  OH. (pp. 21-25)

(2) "For God and Country, Book 2," Copyright 1993 by
  Fr. Paul Link, C.PP.S., "The Messenger Press," Carthagena,
  OH. (pg. 199)

(3) "For God and Country, Book 2," Copyright 1993 by
  Fr. Paul Link, C.PP.S., "The Messenger Press," Carthagena,
  OH. (pg. 202)

(4) "For God and Country, Book 2," Copyright 1993 by
  Fr. Paul Link, C.PP.S., "The Messenger Press," Carthagena,
  OH. (pp. 221-222)

(5) "For God and Country, Book 2," Copyright 1993 by
  Fr. Paul Link, C.PP.S., "The Messenger Press," Carthagena,
  OH. (pg. 240)

(6) "For God and Country, Book 2," Copyright 1993 by
  Fr. Paul Link, C.PP.S., "The Messenger Press," Carthagena,
  OH. (pp. 243-44)

(7) "For God and Country, Book 2," Copyright 1993 by
  Fr. Paul Link, C.PP.S., "The Messenger Press," Carthagena,
  OH. (pg. 247)

(8) "For God and Country, Book 2," Copyright 1993 by
  Fr. Paul Link, C.PP.S., "The Messenger Press," Carthagena,
  OH. (pg.246)

(9) "South American Adventure," Fr. Paul Link C.PP.S.,
  Copyright 1997, "The Messenger Press," Carthagena, OH,
  (pg. 3)

Chapter 13 "The 92nd's Finest Hour"

(1) Scrapbook of Dr. (Capt.) E.F. Pfile of the 92nd Evac. Hospital, containing newspaper clippings from the period 1943-45 from "The Denver Post"

(2) "Tales of the 92nd Evacuation Hospital," brochure printed from Sept., 1993 92nd Reunion at Orlando, FL, containing oral histories of veterans of the 92nd (pp. 53-54)

(3) "For God and Country, Book 2," Copyright 1993 by Fr. Paul Link, C.PP.S., "The Messenger Press," Carthagena, OH. (pg. 244)

(4) "For God and Country, Book 2," Copyright 1993 by Fr. Paul Link, C.PP.S., "The Messenger Press," Carthagena, OH. (pg. 202)

(5) Oral history of Joseph T. Smith

Chapter 14 "Gathering the Scattered Flock"

(1) "For God and Country, Book 2," Copyright 1993 by Fr. Paul Link, C.PP.S., "The Messenger Press," Carthagena, OH. (pg. 240)

(2) "For God and Country, Book 2," Copyright 1993 by Fr. Paul Link, C.PP.S., "The Messenger Press," Carthagena, OH. (pg. 305)

(3) "For God and Country, Book 2," Copyright 1993 by Fr. Paul Link, C.PP.S., "The Messenger Press," Carthagena, OH. (pg. 272)

Chapter 15 "Peace at Last"

(1) "For God and Country, Book 2," Copyright 1993 by Fr. Paul Link, C.PP.S., "The Messenger Press," Carthagena, OH. (pg. 283)

(2) "For God and Country, Book 2," Copyright 1993 by Fr. Paul Link, C.PP.S., "The Messenger Press," Carthagena, OH. (pg. 284)

(3) Oral history of Joseph T. Smith

(4) Excerpt from Fr. Kilian Dreiling's sermon given at 92nd Evac. Reunion, 1977

(5) "For God and Country, Book 2," Copyright 1993 by Fr. Paul Link, C.PP.S., "The Messenger Press," Carthagena, OH. (pg. 311)

(6) "For God and Country, Book 2," Copyright 1993 by Fr. Paul Link, C.PP.S., "The Messenger Press," Carthagena, OH. (pg. 312)

Chapter 16 "Home Sweet Home"

(1) Excerpt from Fr. Kilian Dreiling's sermon at the reunion of the 239th Engineering Battalion, August, 1994

(2) "For God and Country, Book 2," Copyright 1993 by Fr. Paul Link, C.PP.S., "The Messenger Press," Carthagena, OH. (pp. 28-36)

(3) "For God and Country, Book 2," Copyright 1993 by Fr. Paul Link, C.PP.S., "The Messenger Press," Carthagena, OH. (Preface, pg. i")

(4) "South American Adventure," Fr. Paul Link C.PP.S., Copyright 1997, "The Messenger Press," Carthagena, OH, (pp. 3-5)

(5) "Official Service Record" of Fr. Kilian Dreiling, C.PP.S.

Chapter 17 "Return to the Ancestral Homeland"
(1) transcribed from recorded comments made at 92nd Evac. Reunion, Wakeeney, KS, 1977
(2) Oral history of Fr. Kilian Dreiling

Chapter 19 "Civilian Life"
(1) Excerpt from Fr. Kilian Dreiling's sermon at the 92nd Evac. Reunion, Indpls, IN, September, 1983
(2) St. Joseph College, Rensselaer, IN, college yearbook, (circa 1948-50)
(3) "My Story," memoirs of Harry Allagree, installment 4, www.amicicpps.com/harry/harry04.htm
(4) "Official Service Record" of Fr. Kilian Dreiling, C.PP.S.
(5) Letter from Rev. Albert Reed, Jan., 2005
(6) Letter from Rev. Robert L. Connay, Feb., 2005
(7) Letter from Thomas Berschel, Feb., 2005

Chapter 20 "The 'Red-Fighting Priest'"
(1) "Hays Daily News" article, circa August, 1985
(2) Oral history of Fr. Kilian Dreiling

Chapter 22 "The Good Shepherd"
(1) "Official Service Record" of Fr. Kilian Dreiling, C.PP.S.
(2) "Hays Daily News" article, circa August, 1975
(3) Excerpt from Fr. Kilian Dreiling's sermon given at 92nd Evac. Reunion, Orlando, FL, 1993
(4) Oral history of Agnes Pfannenstiel
(5) Euology for Fr. Kilian Dreiling, "New Wine Press," written by Fr. Joe Nassal, January 25, 1997
(6) Letter from Irene Garmann, April 6, 1998
(7) Oral history of Ed Gray

Chapter 23 "Reunion"
(1) Oral history of Agnes Pfannenstiel
(2) 92nd Evac. Reunion newsletter, September, 1975
(3) Transcribed from audio taped conversations from August, 1975
   reunion of 92nd Evac. Hospital. Transcribed by
   Marcella Smith

Chapter 24 "Keeping the Spirit Alive"
(1) "Official Service Record" of Fr. Kilian Dreiling, C.PP.S.
(2) Fr. Kilian Dreiling's Christmas letter, December, 1982
(3) Fr. Kilian Dreiling's Christmas letter, December, 1984
(4) Letter from Fr. Kilian Dreiling to Joseph and Marcella Smith,
   February, 1985
(5) Oral history of Joseph T. Smith
(6) Letter from Fr. Kilian Dreiling to Joseph and Marcella Smith,
   Dec. 23, 1980
(7) Fr. Kilian Dreiling's Christmas letter, December, 1991

Chapter 25 "Embracing Old Age"
(1) "Official Service Record" of Fr. Kilian Dreiling, C.PP.S.
(2) Fr. Kilian Dreiling's Christmas letter, December, 1978
(3) Oral history of Joseph T. Smith